Colin and Faye
When you ...
reminded of God's goodness
I hope this helps.
Grace and peace.
Britt

TIME FOR SUPPER

Smyth & Helwys Publishing, Inc.
6316 Peake Road
Macon, Georgia 31210-3960
1-800-747-3016

Library of Congress Cataloging-in-Publication Data

Younger, Brett, 1961-
Time for supper : invitations to Christ's table / by Brett Younger.
pages cm
ISBN 978-1-57312-720-2 (pbk. : alk. paper)
1. Lord's Supper--Meditations. 2. Church year meditations. I. Title.
BV825.3.Y68 2014
234'.163--dc23

2014016329

BRETT YOUNGER

TIME *for* SUPPER

INVITATIONS TO
CHRIST'S TABLE

Also by Brett Younger

Living with Stress: Nurturing Joy in a Tension-Filled World
(with Carol Younger)

Mark: Finding Ourselves in the Story
(with Carol Younger)

Spirituality: Finding Your Way

Who Moved My Pulpit? A Hilarious Look at Ministerial Life

To Carol,
whose love and grace are gifts of God

ACKNOWLEDGMENTS

I was surprised when he showed up at the church office on Friday morning: "Pastor, I've been charged with possession of cocaine. The story may be in tomorrow's paper. I wanted you to know so that you can line up someone else to serve Communion on Sunday. I don't want to embarrass the church."

I don't understand all of the truth we experience in the Lord's Supper, but I am sure that nothing we can do disqualifies us from a place at the table. The church should be embarrassed if she ever denies anyone the bread and cup.

He served Communion on Sunday. When I got to look him in the eye and say, "This is the cup of forgiveness," it never seemed truer. We come to the table together as a forgiven family.

Any book on the Lord's Supper should be a church project, and this one is. Several congregations have helped me appreciate the grace that we receive at the table: Highland Hills Baptist, Macon, Georgia; First Baptist, Wilmington, North Carolina; First Baptist, Dalton, Georgia; Broadway Baptist, Fort Worth, Texas; Lake Shore Baptist, Waco, Texas; College Heights Baptist, Manhattan, Kansas; and Central Baptist, Paoli, Indiana. Each church taught me to believe in God's overwhelming love.

Thank you to three wonderful McAfee students, Hillary Kimsey, Kate Riney and Jacob Waldrip, who helped with this project. Keith Gammons, Kelley Land and Katie Brookins of Smyth & Helwys edited with grace and forgiveness.

I am most grateful to Carol, who improves what I write with gentle ruthlessness. I am blessed to get to share the table of God's goodness with her.

CONTENTS

Holy Week

Easter

Ordinary Time

INTRODUCTION:
DOING THIS IN
REMEMBRANCE

When I was five years old, we visited my grandmother's church when they were having the Lord's Supper. The worship service had nothing to do with Communion, but after the *long* invitation that closed the service, the preacher said, "It's a fifth Sunday, so we're going to have the Lord's Supper—just like in the Bible."

My parents would not allow me to eat the cracker or drink the thimble of juice for several years, but on this occasion I was sitting with my aunt, whose theology is suspect. When the tray came by, she handed me a broken piece of Saltine and whispered, "Eat it before your mother sees it."

The cracker was fine, but it was the grape juice that I had been eyeing for some time. I couldn't let myself believe that this was finally going to happen, but it did. Aunt Hilma Joyce handed me a shot glass of Welch's. The nectar of the gods tasted even better than I had imagined. It was enough to make you want to be baptized.

Since then I have learned a few things about the theological significance of the Eucharist, but five-year-olds aren't the only ones who don't know exactly what's going on. Why do we call it the celebration of the Lord's Supper when people look sad? If this is supper, why isn't there more food? Some of us ask why the cups are so small and we don't get to drink real wine. What are we supposed to think? How do we need to feel?

The only instruction Jesus gives is "Do this in remembrance of me." We need to remember the story that started it all. In paintings of the Last Supper, Jesus' friends look wise, but the Gospels make it clear that the disciples are several peanuts short of a Snickers.

The biblical writers would like to say that the disciples rise to the occasion, but that is not what happened. Instead, they start bickering about which of them is the greatest. The disciples have every reason to know that something tragic is about to happen, but they jockey for position anyway. Jesus looks at his foolish followers, and we hear the weariness in his voice as he says yet again, "The greatest among you is the one who serves."

At least Peter shows some sign of understanding. "Lord," he says, "I'm ready to die with you."

But Jesus doesn't see much reason to hope in Peter. "You'll deny that you even know me," he tells him.

The table goes silent. Not only will Peter deny him; another of them will actually betray Jesus. "It's the one I give this morsel to," Jesus says as he hands bread to Judas, who immediately slips out into the night.

Jesus picks up the bread and explains, "This is my body."

He breaks it in two and gives it to his disciples. "Take, eat."

Then he holds up the cup. "This is my blood, which is poured out. Drink it."

While the wine still darkens their lips, he says, "I won't drink this again until I drink it with you in my Father's house."

They sing a hymn, but the tune drags like the funeral dirge it is. The disciples gradually remember their way to a tattered courage. God eventually makes saints out of them.

When Elie Wiesel, an Auschwitz survivor who has shared about his experiences through writing and political activism, was asked to summarize all of Holy Scripture in one word, he answered, "Remember."

In the Lord's Supper, we remember. We pretend that the one who breaks the bread and blesses the cup is Jesus. We imagine that bread and juice are flesh and blood and that, by swallowing them, we swallow God's grace into our lives.

Maybe the meal Jesus ate with his disciples should be called the First Supper rather than the last. It was the first of many times that

Christians have gathered for this meal to remember that God is with us. We remember not part of the past but the evidence of the present—not God who is gone but God who is here.

We eat the bread and remember a love beyond anything we practice. We meet God at the table and see ourselves more honestly. We see how we ignore hurting people by doing what is safe. We are quick to join negative conversations and slow to speak positive words. We become too preoccupied with our own agendas to remember Christ's story.

We drink the cup to remember that we need God because we cannot make it on our own. We need God to teach us to give, because we do not share well. We need God to make us kind, because we are not as caring as we should be. We need God to show us how to love, because we do not love enough.

One of my minimum-wage jobs during seminary was as a maintenance worker at an evangelical church. My favorite part of the work was setting up for the Lord's Supper service each Friday evening. The building was quiet on Friday afternoons. The only other person working was Larry—a good-hearted, mentally challenged custodian.

Preparing the elements became my time of prayer. One Friday was particularly holy. As I took bread and grape juice from the refrigerator and set them on the counter, I thought about how amazing it is that these elements become so important. For two thousand years, Christians have been taking bread and cup and remembering.

As I set up chairs, I thought about those who would participate. Would they realize how much they are like the first disciples? Would they be awake enough to be humbled?

As I hooked up the microphone, I put myself in the place of the leader who would say, "This bread is my body broken for you." How can you say that without a lump in your throat?

I reverently walked back to the kitchen to find my high holy moment shattered. Larry was chug-a-lugging the blood of Jesus. I grew angry for a moment, but then I realized something. Larry and that irreverently tilted mug of Welch's define the word *preposterous*, but my place at the table is just as preposterous. What could be more preposterous than people like us sharing in the goodness of God? What could be more surprising than grace that pours itself out for us?

Some argue that every meal in literature is a Communion scene. Could every meal in the Bible or even every biblical text be a Communion text? The Lord's Supper is betrayal in the upper room, but it is also dinner in Emmaus and breakfast by the Sea of Tiberias. The themes of the Eucharist are sorrow and hunger, and also joy and nourishment. At the Lord's table, we experience gratitude, friendship, forgiveness, and sacrifice.

Time for Supper: Invitations to Christ's Table is a Christian year of fifty-two invitations to Communion. These meditations on the Lord's Supper are meant to help us listen to the myriad of ways God invites us to gratefully, reverently, and joyfully chug-a-lug the cup of Christ.

Advent

AN INVITATION TO HOPE

MARK 13:24-37

"Keep awake—for you do not know when the owner of the house will come, in the evening, or at midnight, or at cockcrow, or at dawn, or else the owner may find you asleep when he comes suddenly." (Mark 13:35-36)

A good friend works hard to keep me informed by sending op-ed pieces from the *New York Times*, articles from *Christian Century*, and Texas Aggie jokes. Every now and then, he sends an update from the Rapture Index at www.raptureready.com. The purpose of this website is to "eliminate the wide variance that currently exists with prophecy reporting" and compile the information into a "cohesive indicator." The Rapture Index is a "Dow Jones of end times, a prophetic speedometer. The higher the number the faster we're moving towards the rapture."

These people, who seem to have too much time on their hands as they wait for the end of time, list forty-five categories to which they assign a score of one to five. Indicators of the end of the world include the occult, Satanism, false prophets, the mark of the beast, the Antichrist, earthquakes, floods, plagues, unemployment, inflation, interest rates, globalism, ecumenism, liberalism, and civil rights. Civil rights? The scale for the total score ranges from below 85—"slow prophetic activity"—to above 145—"fasten your seat belt." The last time I checked, the rapture index was 164. Stay calm.

The goofiness that surrounds the Second Coming of Christ is embarrassing. One of the clearest things Jesus said was, "No one knows the day or hour" (Mark 13:32). Fortunetellers have been guessing the day and hour ever since.

In 1000 CE, a flurry of predictions led many Christians to sell their homes. Martin Luther said that the Pope was the Antichrist, so he expected Jesus to be back soon. Christopher Columbus thought that his explorations would lead to the final crusade. William Miller predicted that the Second Coming would take place in 1843. Miller's followers, the Seventh Day Adventists, have since adjusted their schedule. Charles Taze Russell, founder of the Jehovah's Witnesses, predicted that the apocalypse would happen in 1914. This group, too, has postponed the end of the world.

The best-selling religious book of the 1970s was Hal Lindsey's *The Late Great Planet Earth*. The author predicted that Jesus would return in the next few years. He spent profits from the book on a mansion that took three years to build.

When I was in junior high, an evangelist came to our church and said that Jesus would be back in less than five years. Every thirteen-year-old boy had the same thought: "I will never get to have sex." As the year 2000 approached, people began finding references to "Y2K" in the book of Revelation. The *Left Behind* series made huge money in spite of the kid from *Growing Pains* starring in the movie version. The Mayans put their money on 2012.

The silliness surrounding the Second Coming seems as outdated as handwritten letters, real country music, and Mel Gibson's career. Good church members are tempted to ignore the Second Coming altogether.

But the early Christians also believed that the end of the world was around the corner. The Gospel of Mark was written forty years after Jesus' death, just after the Romans destroyed the temple in Jerusalem. Mark wrote to tell persecuted Christians about how, two days before he died, Jesus told his friends about the end of it all.

If you were describing the end of time, what kind of language would you use? Would you use scientific language? Would you use theological language? Or would you use the kind of apocalyptic language Jesus used? Maybe you would use words like these: "When things are at their most horrible, when it is worse than you can imagine, when the sun does not shine, the moon goes black, the stars fall from the sky, and creation falls apart, know that God is coming for you. The whole universe will melt away like a dream, and something new—something it never entered your head to imagine—will come crashing in."

Jesus said that we can know God is coming in the same way a fig tree knows summer is coming (Mark 13:28). The change of seasons can be seen in the tree's softening branches and sprouting leaves. We can feel God's coming in the softening of our hearts. In Jesus' parable, the sign of God's coming is not the catastrophe that some look for; it is the hope that stirs within our spirits.

Jesus told another story that probably gave the disciples insomnia (vv. 34-36). A master goes on a trip and leaves the servants to manage the house. They need to be on the lookout constantly, because though the master may have marked the date on his calendar, he decided not to share that information with his servants.

Any teenager who has ever been left in charge of the house knows how good the first few moments feel. The whole house is yours. You can eat what you want and leave your clothes on the floor. Of course, eventually the work you were given to do starts to nag at you. The dishes pile up. The plants need watering. You have to clean up the mess. Sooner or later, you have to get to it.

I saw a T-shirt that read, "Jesus is coming. Look busy." But this parable tells us to actually *get busy* and *pay attention*. As you vacuum, keep watching for the car in the driveway. As you pick up items in the living room, listen to hear the front door open. None of us ever know when the end will come—for us, for those we love, or for the world.

Jesus kept saying, "Don't take anything for granted. God could show up any time."

If you fall asleep for fifteen minutes, you might miss the most important moment of your life. You might wake up to find God standing over you with luggage in both hands saying, "Where were you when I arrived? The door was wide open, and there were no lights on. I told you to stay awake."

Wake up and understand that what we believe about the future affects the way we live each day. When we look for God's coming, we hear the ticking of the clock and understand that every minute is filled with hope and despair. Our job is to stay awake to everything that life brings us—so that we do not miss God when God comes.

Believing that the end belongs to God breaks the power of the world and fills us with a hope that continues even in sorrow. Woodrow Wilson said, "It's better to struggle as part of a movement that will ultimately succeed than to succeed in a movement that will ultimately fail." If we believe that God will win, then sorrow is less permanent.

In New York City, there is a church with a statue of the angel Gabriel on the roof. His horn is lifted to his mouth, ready to blow a mighty blast to announce God's coming. Day after day, Gabriel stands ready. Warmed by the summer sun, frozen by winter sleet, year after year goes by, but no mighty blast comes—not even a tentative toot. The streets of the city below are crawling with traffic, lined with apartments and businesses. Birth, death, love, conflict, and a thousand shattered hopes take place between dawn and sunset every day. To most of the people on the street, Gabriel must seem silly.

But the biggest questions remain. To what are we heading? Who will have the final word? What is going to happen?

The bread at Christ's table reminds us that we are not alone and that God is caring for us. We know of promises casually broken, but we drink the cup of God's faithfulness.

On the days when we feel so good that we wish it would last forever, and on the days when we feel so bad that we wish time would end right then, the table offers the same promise. God is waiting at the end of it all.

AN INVITATION TO PEACE

JEREMIAH 33:14-16

In those days and at that time I will cause a righteous Branch to spring up for David; and he shall execute justice and righteousness in the land. (Jeremiah 33:15)

The signs for the beginning of the Christmas season—decorations in the stores, carols on the radio, and trees in the parking lots—show up before Halloween. By the time December arrives, we are in the middle of the Christmas season. By the first week of Advent, retailers are running out of walkie-talkie wristwatches, Let's Rock Elmos, and head massagers. Pay attention in November, or you may miss *A Charlie Brown Christmas.*

In cynical moments, we wonder if Christmas is the season for wishful thinking. In December, we act as if the world is better than it is. We think more kindly of others. Families pretend that they get along better than they actually do. At some of our gatherings, certain people are expected to keep their distance. They are not exactly unwanted, but they are only around at Christmas and are not the first ones invited. At some gatherings, you will be the last one invited, and you will not even know it. Throughout the Christmas season, we are expected to act happier than we really are.

Even though we recognize the superficiality of much that is associated with the holidays, December is still the best time of the year for many. Maybe what we're doing is not just pretending but rehearsing. Because we recognize that the world is not what it should be, we enjoy acting as though it is.

We need to rehearse for a better day. Christmas, Advent, and praying for peace matter most when we recognize how much we need God's peace.

In spite of the festivities, the world has rejected the Prince of Peace. We are never without multiple major military conflicts. Most of these are civil wars fueled by racial, ethnic, or religious animosity. Most victims are civilians. During World War I, civilians made up fewer than 5 percent of casualties. Today, more than 75 percent of those killed in wars are noncombatants.

Africa, to a greater extent than any other continent, is afflicted by war, marred by more than twenty major civil wars since 1960. Rwanda, Somalia, Angola, Sudan, Liberia, and Burundi have suffered serious armed conflict. Food production is impossible in war-torn areas, and famine often results. Conflict condemns children to lives of misery. Yet throughout the world, statues of war heroes fill our parks. We do not have many monuments to peace heroes.

In the midst of a terrible war, Jeremiah cursed the day he was born, and you can hardly blame him. The prophet spent his whole life telling the Hebrew people to shape up, but they remained just as miserable as they would have been if he had never bothered. Jerusalem was falling apart. Like many cities, it had become a violent place. The armies of Nebuchadnezzar had demolished most of the city, tearing down the temple, stealing the best stuff, and taking the best people. For warning them ahead of time, Jeremiah was charged with treason. As he wrote his text, Jeremiah was in jail.

The best that can be said about despair is that it leads to hope. To see the stars in the highest heavens, we must sit for a while in the darkness on earth. Through our waiting, we long for the final Advent of peace.

We wait for something beyond what we can do on our own. One attorney explained the limits of the judicial process: "Our American legal system does a good job within a limited sphere. Our courts can apply the rules to give you some remuneration for your pain, some compensatory aid for your troubles, but we cannot give you justice. Too many people leave the courts angry because they asked for too much. They asked for justice. We can give you money, we can punish a criminal or two, but we can't set things right."

Advent is about justice. Advent is God setting things right in a way that we will never accomplish on our own. When Jeremiah proclaims God's promise of a "righteous Branch to spring up for David," he addresses our deepest longings. Jeremiah speaks this word of hope in a moment that seems hopeless. The promise of God appears in the bleakest times, as if one of the requirements for God's peace is recognizing the horror of war. The peace for which we wait is shining in the distance.

Jeremiah does not say anything about people making their own lives better. Peace is not dependent on the meager peace that we can and should share, but on God coming with peace that will last forever.

Harriet Beecher Stowe said, "The longest day must have its close—the gloomiest night will wear on to a morning. An eternal, inexorable lapse of moments is ever hurrying the day of the evil to an eternal night, and the night of the just to an eternal day."

We will suffer battles, but at the end of it all, God will end the wars and bring peace. The promise is that when all has been said and done, in us as individuals, in our political, social, and economic structures, and in the whole creation, God will finally reign.

The good news of Advent is that God will not give up on the world. We are being transformed by a revolutionary God who intends to make all things new. So we live as if the world is a little better than it is. We prepare for a better day by living more like the Christ who has come. We love God in friends, enemies, neighbors, strangers, homeless, and hopeless. We live in the hope of peace.

God is waiting to fill empty spirits with joy, give us the courage to risk, and invite us to love. We open our hearts to the boundless future that is already coming. We share the supper as a celebration of the peace that is yet to be. Jesus' birth calls us to be born again, Jesus' suffering and death invite us to die to sin, and Jesus' resurrection is the promise of peace. We live with hope for all the possibilities in heaven and on earth.

An Invitation to Joy

Mark 1:1-8

The beginning of the good news of Jesus Christ, the Son of God. As it is written in the prophet Isaiah, "See, I am sending my messenger ahead of you, who will prepare your way." (Mark 1:1-2)

If we relied on Mark, we would have to stretch to get a story worth a Christmas carol. The Gospel of Mark does not begin like Matthew, Luke, or John. Mark has no shepherds keeping watch over their flocks by night, no Mary, no Joseph, no manger, no wise men, no Herod, no "In the beginning was the Word," and no baby Jesus. Mark either does not know the stories of Jesus' birth or does not think they are important enough to keep in the final draft.

Mark starts his Gospel with a wild man in the desert: "This is the beginning of the good news of Jesus Christ, the Child of God. Isaiah wrote, 'See, I'm sending my messenger ahead of you, a socially, religiously, politically incorrect prophet.'"

John is the voice crying in the wilderness, the honking horn, and the buzzing alarm clock. He wears animal skins and smells of honey-dipped locusts. John has never seen the inside of a barbershop. His tumbleweed hairdo makes Willie Nelson look well groomed.

John's popularity is hard to figure. Would you have gone to hear him? Would you have paid attention to John the Baptist for even five minutes? While he sounds like the street preachers who tell you that you are going to hell on the next bus if you do not repent right now, there is a big difference between John and most street preachers. Self-appointed prophets tend to plant themselves in your way so that you have to cross to the other side of the street to avoid them. John set up shop in the wilderness, and anyone who wanted to hear him had to go to a lot of trouble to get there. John is not speaking at the Convention Center. He is six miles east of a one-stop-sign town, four miles south on a dirt road, two miles east on a footpath, and another half-mile north off the path. Why would anyone make a trip like that to hear a sermon? The temple was in Jerusalem. The preachers were there. If someone wanted to hear about God, they could attend a few services and join a Bible study.

John is as far away from the temple as he can get. The people flock to John because he is *not* part of the religious establishment. Only those willing to go into the wilderness and think outside the usual expectations are able to know the Spirit that is beyond what religion offers.

John was hard for religious people to take because he told the truth. He told them to wake up, follow the Spirit, and start doing what God wanted to do with them. John was executed for his honesty.

John tells people to "repent," not as a resolution to do better but as a way of seeing everything differently. Those who listened to John understood that repentance means turning away from everything that denies hope and turning toward everything that leads to joy. People went to the wilderness to hear John because he invited them to travel a new road, to stop meeting expectations and try something new.

John did not have any credentials other than his belief that baptism was the hope of beginning again. He baptized women who were not allowed to sit in the best seats in the temple. He baptized sinners who were never invited to eat with good people. He baptized high school seniors and middle-aged ministers. John baptized everyone who wanted to start again.

John the Baptist does not make it into the Christmas pageant for good reasons. "You brood of vipers. Who warned you to flee from the wrath to come?" does not make it onto Christmas cards. John did not get invited to many parties, but his message is at the heart of the season. Christmas is about God offering the gift of something more.

In some ways, the Christian faith is center stage at Christmas celebrations, but this season also points out the differences between

Christians and culture. Reading the Christmas story in the Bible and finding connections to the ways we usually celebrate Christmas is hard.

We feel the tension between hyper-consumerism and the baby born in a stable. We do not want to believe that the more we spend, the more fun we will have. We do not want our children to think that they have to have what everyone else is getting, but coming up with an alternative way of celebrating seems like work. Who has time to make gifts, write poems, and adapt Martha Stewart's plans to construct our own Chrismons? December never turns out like we hope. So it is common for churches to denounce the secularization of Christmas—"Remember the reason for the season."

Ministers preach scathing critiques of the commercialization of Christmas, calling believers to focus on its spiritual meaning. The next day, those same preachers drive to Target to buy Barbie Designable Hair Extensions and Ultimate Optimus Prime Transformers. The trappings that surround Christmas almost cover the hope for something holy.

Christmas is the chance to live in God's hope. If we ask, "What will Christmas look like if we really believe that God is with us?" then Christmas will look different. We will not let agenda anxiety keep us from remembering that there are those whom God loves who do not have the resources to celebrate; for some, there are no gifts because they are poor; for some, there is no joy because they are broken in spirit; for some, there is no family because they have no one.

If we believe that God is with us, we will have a more meaningful Christmas. Feel the joy of Christmas as it is *and* the joy of what could be. Love our children *and* other people's children, too. Give to people we love *and* to people we have never met. Remember happy memories *and* make new ones. Think about Jesus in the manger *and* about God who is with us now.

We will not have a Christmas as holy as the one we imagine. We will never get Christmas completely right, and that is okay. The tension we feel in December is the tension we feel all year long. We know that we could be better than we are. Trying something new may lead to frustration, but it also leads to wonder.

Igor Stravinsky had written a new piece with a difficult violin passage. After the orchestra had rehearsed for several weeks, the solo violinist came to Stravinsky and said that he was sorry, he had tried his best, but the passage was too difficult. No violinist could play it. Stravinsky replied, "I understand that. What I'm after is the sound of someone *trying* to play it."

God is pleased with the sound of God's children *trying* to play in a new way. Christmas is a time to start caring for the hurting, become more of who we should be, and understand that we live in the presence of God.

We come to the table thanking God for the gift of Christ's coming. We come not as angels but as saints and sinners. Where we sorrow, God brings joy; where we are apathetic, God invites us to love; where we fail, God offers grace.

An Invitation to the Kingdom

Isaiah 11:1-10

The spirit of the LORD shall rest on him,
the spirit of wisdom and understanding,
the spirit of counsel and might,
the spirit of knowledge and the fear of the LORD.
(Isaiah 11:2)

The news that the world is going to be turned upside down is good news or bad news depending on where you happen to be standing when you hear it. If the world seems easy, pleasant, and safe, then the announcement that God is bringing a different world is threatening. If you live in grief, poverty, and sadness, then a new world is definitely good news.

In 1988, amid the struggles against racism in South Africa, when it looked like the forces of apartheid would prevail, Archbishop Desmond Tutu preached to the leaders of his country, "You may be powerful, indeed very powerful, but you are not God. You are ordinary mortals. God, the God whom we worship, cannot be mocked. You have already lost. We are inviting you to come and join the winning side."

The problem is that when it is difficult to feel anything but despair, believing that you are on the winning side is hard.

The Hebrew people were on a long losing streak. The poet Isaiah says that they were as dead as a tree stump in West Texas. Short and bare, a stump was all that remained after an ax did its work. Once upon a time, a majestic oak stood there. Birds could build nests. Trees held swing sets. A stump means no more shade from the sun, no more safe haven for birds, no more swing sets. However strong the tree might have been, it had no chance when the ax showed up.

Judah was reduced to a lifeless stump. The great kingdom of David once strong and majestic has been chopped down. With corrupt leaders who loved bribes and ignored the needy, the mighty kingdom fell. Israel, the northern portion, had already been taken, and Judah was on the brink of deportation.

Isaiah sees a day when the temple will be gone, the walls of Jerusalem rubble, and nothing left of the people of Abraham, Moses, and David. What *is* there looks like a stump compared to what once was.

This is not how we would say it, but who has not felt like a stump, like a tree that has been knocked over, like our best days are over, like the good that once was is no more?

A stump looks like losing someone we love. Many of us grieve for people who were part of our lives but have now chosen not to be. Broken relationships cause an aching void, leaving anger, fear, and hurt.

Our jobs can feel like a dead end. The work we do doesn't matter. We dread the sound of the alarm clock each morning. Many people have way too much work that doesn't need to be done. We end up hardened by what we think we have to do.

We live with endings and disappointments. A battle is going on between despair and faith. When we spend our days remembering what used to be, we need a new vision.

The poet catches a glimpse of hope. Out of this dead stump, Isaiah sees a shoot, a branch so insignificant that it goes unnoticed. Out of the stump of Jesse, the father of David, the unexpected shepherd king, there is hope for a new king who will defeat the mighty Goliaths.

He will be a genuine leader, filled with the spirit of wisdom and understanding. The new king will not be open to bribes ("what his eyes see") or convinced by propaganda ("what his ears hear"). This king will not sit back and let market forces dictate who gets too much and who gets nothing. He will care for those who are left out.

Isaiah imagines that in place of the usual weapons of military office—sword and spear—this king will be dressed in the regalia of love and compassion. He will not be the puppet of the pollsters and the powerful, but a leader with heart and spirit.

Isaiah 11 was a coronation psalm written for a particular king, but Isaiah's imagination gets away from him as he goes beyond the range of human possibility and sees a peaceable kingdom. Wolves will play with lambs. Leopards will sleep next to goats. Calves and lions will eat from the same trough. A little child will laugh with rattlesnakes. This is more than King David or Gunther Gebel-Williams could pull off.

Arabs and Jews from the Middle East, Catholics and Protestants from Northern Ireland, pro-life and pro-choice, Gay Pride and Focus on the Family, the National Rifle Association and the American Civil Liberties Union, Jon Stewart and Bill O'Reilly will break bread together. And a little child will lead them.

This would be unbelievable poetry, except that we have heard the story. We have seen the king of whom Isaiah dreamed. At the darkest moment, like a tender green shoot coming out of a disintegrating tree trunk, in the tiny village of Bethlehem, seven pounds, twenty inches or so. Hope so tiny he is easy to miss.

You wonder if Isaiah would have recognized him. Jesus was a different kind of king. He ruled with stories. He walked to work and slept beneath the stars. He lived among the poor and called them neighbor. He filled his calendar with people whom kings have no time for. He refused the kingdoms of this world.

Jesus talked about the kingdom as a great banquet, a hidden treasure, a pearl of great price; a kingdom where the prodigal and his brother celebrate; a kingdom for widows and orphans, the sick and lonely; a kingdom where families reconcile after years of shutting each other out; where our work is to care for the earth; where the fellowship of the church is as wide as the grace of God; where there is joy for those who thought they would never laugh again and hope for those who feel like they are disintegrating.

Even when our hearts feel dead, God stirs us in tiny ways that are easy to miss. God brings life when you smile at a tired clerk. You choose not to enter into a battle for position in a line of traffic. You help your child with her homework instead of turning on the television. You read the paper and quietly say a prayer for peace.

You notice that, without thinking about it too much, you have forgiven someone. You speak a word of kindness to a person you never liked and think, "Where did that come from?"

You stop the normal routine and do something surprising. You laugh out loud and know that the joke was not that funny. You wake up in the morning and see it as a chance to start again.

You feel Christ with you, the hope that overcomes our fears. When the baby born in Bethlehem grew up, he offered an example of focusing more on loving than on being loved, more on forgiving than on being forgiven, more on understanding than on being understood. Christ's hope sounded threatening, so the ax was laid to the tree once more, nails to the cross. Jesus was dead as a tree stump, but God brought new life.

In Christ, God invades our despair and offers the way of faith. At Christ's table, we give ourselves again. When our world is crashing down around us, the table helps us remember hope.

Christmas

HOME FOR CHRISTMAS

LUKE 2:1-7

And she gave birth to her firstborn son and wrapped him in bands of cloth, and laid him in a manger because there was no place for them in the inn. (Luke 2:7)

More of us have memories of Christmas Eve than of any other night of the year. Nostalgia and expectation fill the air. According to Clement Moore, children nestle "all snug in their beds while visions of sugarplums dance in their heads," but not many children actually dream of sugarplums—or know what they are. Yet even those of us who think we are beyond magic and wonder will, if we are paying any attention, feel magic and wonder on Christmas Eve, at least for a moment.

Children come home from college for a few days. Children come home from some place far away that took our sons or daughters just as they were beginning to be fun to have around. Children come home with significant others whom we suspect are not good enough for them.

What makes Christmas wonderful is the feeling of going home. Many of my Christmases were spent in Mantachie, Mississippi, at my grandparents' house. The women were in the kitchen preparing the meal. The men were in the living room talking about hunting and fishing. If it wasn't too cold, the children were in the front yard playing and, every now and then, taking turns riding "Old Lady," the only horse we could ride unsupervised. When she really got going, Old Lady could go two or three miles an hour. If it was cold, my cousins and I were usually in the middle bedroom, which had a radio. We surreptitiously participated in the devil's pastime. We played cards while listening carefully for the sound of my grandmother coming to check on us. Teenagers today smoke crack cocaine with less fear than I felt while playing Old Maid.

Before Christmas dinner, Grandpa prayed a long prayer in which he thanked God for everyone at the table. We always took a couple of hours to recover from dinner and then gathered around a tree that had too many stringy silver icicles. One of the children read the Christmas story from Luke before we could open any gifts. The other children wanted the story read faster. The connection between Jesus and the presents was not clear.

We thought the gifts were a big deal, but they weren't much— sparklers, baseballs, completely unappreciated pairs of socks. We received stockings filled with fruit for which none of us cared one bit. My mother made divinity—our version of sugarplums.

My childhood Christmas memories are of feeling at home. I'm sure it was not as good as I remember it, but most of what we do at Christmas is an attempt to feel the warmth of being home.

Even people who have never had a good home carry a vision of Christmas within them. Christmas is longing to belong. We want to love and be loved.

Our longing for home leads us to the manger. Home is the destination for a worried father-to-be making his way to Bethlehem with his expectant fiancée. Under unimaginable conditions, a child is born to this young mother, barely more than a child herself. She wraps her boy in swaddling clothes and lays him in a feed trough, nestling him in the hay.

Home is where the hopes and fears of all of our years meet. We long for home like Mary and Joseph longed for home. We long to come home like shepherds to kneel and give thanks. We are homesick people who long for homemade bread and a cup of cheer. We long for the home we taste and see in Christ's coming.

CATCHING A GLIMPSE

LUKE 2:22-38

Now there was a man in Jerusalem whose name was Simeon; this man was righteous and devout, looking forward to the consolation of Israel, and the Holy Spirit rested on him. It had been revealed to him by the Holy Spirit that he would not see death before he had seen the Lord's Messiah. (Luke 2:25-26)

The first Christmas comes and goes, and most people don't notice. Mary, Joseph, the shepherds, and a few others catch a glimpse of what is happening, but they're just a handful. Bethlehem is so crowded that the hope of the world is born, and most miss it.

Simeon is not going to miss it. He has been waiting a long time. Simeon has a feeling that he will not die until he has seen the Messiah. He spends his days in the sanctuary running after every woman who carries a blue blanket. When Simeon catches up with them, the young mothers smile and ask, "Would you like to see my baby?"

Simeon tries not to look disappointed. "I'm sorry. I thought he might be somebody else."

The holy family, who would not have referred to themselves as the holy family, goes to Jerusalem for the baby's dedication. The shepherds, angels, and heavenly hosts are long gone. Mary and Joseph have been left with a son to raise. Jesus is two months old, still keeping them up at night.

With both hope and helplessness, Mary and Joseph carry their tiny stranger through the temple.

Simeon asks the pastoral assistant, "What's on the schedule this morning?"

"You have a counseling session with the Rabinowitz boy and his fiancée at eleven. Oh, and there's a baby waiting to be dedicated. His name is Jesus."

"Jesus, you say?"

"Simeon, this is no royal birth. His father is a carpenter. You've dedicated hundreds of babies and dozens named Jesus. *What makes you think this one is different? And what makes you think you would recognize the Messiah if you saw him?*"

"But how can I stop believing? The hope keeps me going, so if I chase strollers around the temple, humor me."

When it's her turn, Mary steps forward, presenting her child to be blessed by the ancient rabbi.

Then Simeon looks at Jesus, and his heart begins to race. He knows. He is not sure if he should laugh or cry.

"May I hold the baby?" he asks Mary, trembling as he holds out his arms.

Cradling the child, with tears streaming down his cheeks, Simeon says the most astonishing thing: "Now I can pass away in peace. This is the hope we've been waiting for."

Years will pass, and Simeon will pass away long before this child shares a word of God's grace, feeds the hungry, or calls would-be followers. Simeon beholds only the beginning of the promise, but it is enough. Like a slave addressing his king, Simeon asks to be dismissed: "God, you can release your servant, for these old eyes have seen your salvation."

Imagine expecting "gitchy gitchy goo" and getting "This child will be the light of revelation for all people." Joseph is tongue-tied. Mary does not know how to take the part about her heart being pierced with a sword. The two of them spend the rest of their days not quite sure how to respond. Simeon does not understand everything either, but he knows hope when he sees it.

We are usually too distracted to recognize God's presence. We spend most days preparing for the next day, treating our present circumstances as stepping stones. But this place and this hour are the only place and hour available in which we can make a place for God. The sacred wish at the depths of our hearts, the wondrous hope that we rarely think about, is *God with us.*

At the Lord's table, we glimpse our salvation. The supper is an opportunity to recognize God's presence and give ourselves over to hope.

Epiphany

SEEKING WISDOM

MATTHEW 2:1-12

In the time of King Herod, after Jesus was born in Bethlehem of Judea, magi from the East came to Jerusalem, asking, "Where is the child who has been born king of the Jews?" (Matthew 2:1-2)

Smart people are open to wisdom wherever they find it. A newspaper asked children and teenagers to send in their deepest thoughts.

This is wisdom from a six-year-old: "For centuries, people thought the moon was made of green cheese. Then the astronauts found that the moon is really a big hard rock. That's what happens to cheese when you leave it out."

An eight-year-old wrote, "It sure would be nice if we got a day off for the President's birthday, like they do for the Queen. Of course, then we would have a lot of people voting for a candidate born on July 3 or December 26, just for the long weekends."

Here's some fifteen-year-old wisdom: "I believe you should live each day as if it is your last, which is why I don't have any clean laundry, because who wants to wash clothes on the last day of their life?"

We should be open to wisdom wherever we find it. Many mistakenly limit their search to what can be seen and measured. For them, only the facts are worthy of attention. The intellectual is viewed in opposition to the spiritual. Some people quickly dismiss anything that smacks of the sacred.

Atheists argue that science has made religion unnecessary, but their arguments are not convincing. The fact that nature obeys precise mathematical laws, that life emerged from inanimate matter, and that the universe exists are best explained by a God who works beyond what we can see and measure.

Skeptics sound like they are trying to convince themselves that life can have meaning without God, but without God, life is without Spirit. To choose skepticism is to miss the truths of faith and spirituality. Cynicism leads to a view of life that is ultimately despairing.

The truly wise leave their minds open to possibilities farther out and deeper within. We should imagine more than we can explain, confess that we need to believe, and admit our sense of the sacred. We should look for the wisdom of the Spirit.

In many of the Gospel stories, Jesus goes looking for people, intrudes into their lives, and moves into their villages. In Matthew's story of the magi, though, they come looking for Jesus. No one travels farther to see him than they do.

Matthew calls them "magi," not "wise men" or "kings." The word *magi* is the root from which we get "magician." A magus was a sorcerer and a scientist, an astrologer and astronomer, a physicist and physician and metaphysicist, too. Science and superstition were not yet separated, and the magi dabbled in all of it.

With their star charts and whatever passed for telescopes fifteen hundred years before telescopes, the magi in Matthew come to the peculiar conclusion that a new king has been born in Israel.

They come looking for wisdom, but we don't know much else about the wise men, so we have made stuff up.

One early tradition is that there were twelve magi, but that made the crèche crowded. Since there were three gifts, shaky evidence though it is, we went with three wise men.

There may have been women in the group. Apparently, they got lost and stopped to ask for directions.

One legend is that the journey took thirty days. A trip like that was uncommon—such a long distance, sore-footed camels, unfriendly towns, dangerous bandits, the uncertainty of what lay behind the next sand dune.

An unexplainable longing sends the magi on this unreasonable trip. They arrive in Jerusalem and start asking, "Where can we find the newborn King of the Jews? We saw a star that signaled his birth. We've come to worship him."

When Herod hears the news, he gets nervous. Herod is a fake king of the Jews, put in power by the Romans. He fears for his job. He asks the reference librarians for help.

Six hundred years earlier, Isaiah wrote about a pilgrimage of rich kings to Jerusalem, riding a multitude of camels and bringing gifts of gold and frankincense. The psalmist wrote of kings falling down before the Messiah who would deliver the needy and the poor. The prophet Micah gave directions: "It's you, Bethlehem. From you will come the shepherd for God's people."

Herod's scribes are smart enough to quote Micah but not wise enough to look for the child themselves.

Herod suggests that the wise men conduct a thorough search and check back: "When you find him, come back, be my guest, and I'll go worship him also. We kings have to stick together."

The magi set off, the star appears, and they throw the most famous baby shower ever. They can hardly contain themselves. Mary and Joseph are confused, but the magi celebrate because they have found their way to the long-awaited hope.

They open their treasures and worship. Matthew doesn't give us details. The magi's visit lasts one verse. We are not told if they stayed for dinner, what they thought, what they felt, or if Mary traded the myrrh for diapers.

The magi are out of place in this humble village, like the Dalai Lama showing up unannounced in Utah. Gentiles rather than Jews followed the star, but Christ waits for anyone who looks for wisdom.

God calls us to the wisdom that will help us be more than we are. The baby whom the magi found was the beginning of the journey. We do not merely *believe* in Jesus. We *follow* Jesus. Christ takes us to places that we would not have gone without his leading. We have a desert to travel, a star to discover, and life to be found.

Our trivial desires threaten to obscure our genuine longing. God gently tries to persuade us to turn our attention from the temporary to the permanent—from passing time to investing in eternity.

Are we courageous enough to seek God's wisdom? Are we willing to relinquish our control and go where Christ leads us? Can we rise to a new sense of adventure, forsake our cozy boundaries, and follow Christ?

The wise men wanted to see Jesus more than they wanted to keep their treasures, more than they wanted to play it safe, and more than they feared the difficulties of the journey.

The deepest wisdom leads us to give ourselves to God in the bread and cup. The table is for those who are seeking wisdom. The supper is the promise that the world we know best, the world of Herod, the world of fear, is giving way to the world we seek, the world of hope.

RISE AND SHINE

Arise, shine; for your light has come, and the glory of the
LORD has risen upon you. (Isaiah 60:1)

An atheist was upset with me. I had written to the *Fort Worth Star-Telegram*, responding to an article about the growing number of people with no religious affiliation who consider themselves spiritual. I gently suggested that spirituality without God is empty, and that what many people who claim to be spiritual without going to church really want is to be spiritual without taking responsibility. I implied that some use their lack of faith in the church as an excuse not to give money to the needy or work for social justice. I argued that true spirituality leads people to feed the hungry, listen to the lonely, and join with others who are doing the same.

What I wrote made perfect sense to me, but a self-described "hard-core atheist" in Colorado sent an e-mail informing me that I am "painfully ignorant." I have grown accustomed to a certain level of ignorance, but "painfully ignorant" sounds rather negative. He helpfully pointed out that those who attend church can be just as greedy, cheap, and unfeeling as those who do not. This is not news to a Baptist preacher. He also wrote that he hoped my next sermon would better reflect the truth.

One of the disadvantages of e-mailing ministers is that it is easier for us to send a sermon than a thoughtful response. I attached a sermon on why it makes sense to believe in God, and the debate was on.

My atheist friend responded with a lengthy rebuttal he would give
if offered the opportunity to speak at my church—an offer that was
not forthcoming. He and I covered heaven, hell, prayer, faith-healing,
easy answers, difficult questions, astronomy, awe, skepticism, curiosity,
the Old Testament, the New Testament, the death penalty, black
holes, quantum gravity, warped space-time, fifteen billion years of
evolution, Carl Sagan, Jerry Falwell, and which one of us had the
worse experience in Sunday school.

As you would guess, neither one of us changed the other's mind.
My atheist pen pal wants verifiable proof—"no evidence, no belief"
is how he put it. Ultimately, I have to admit that what I hold is
impossible to prove. I believe that once in a while I see a glimmer of
light. That is not much to go on.

Isaiah could not prove that he had seen a flash of light in the
middle of a stormy night. The prophet lived in dark times. An enemy
army wiped out Jerusalem, the temple, and the economy of once-
proud Judah. The tiny remnant of Israel, those who were not killed
or carried off to Babylon, was again threatened with destruction.
Palestine was forever being overrun. Wars between the countries to
the east and west brought foreign armies to Israel. When battles took
place, Hebrew parents watched their children being carried away. The
days were dark because the people's hearts were far from God. No one
paid attention to anyone who thought that God mattered.

In the middle of the night, the prophet Isaiah saw a light. "Rise
and shine!" Isaiah shouted. "Get out of bed. God is here. Jerusalem is
in ashes, but just when it looks like the sun will never rise again, dawn
is about to break: Your sons will return from far away, and your
daughters will be carried in their mothers' arms again. The sight of
the exiles coming home will make your face break out in a grin, your
heart pound, and your eyes light up. The whole world will come
riding camels and bringing gifts. People will march in from the South
and sail in from the West. They will bring gold and frankincense, bow
down, and worship God's light."

Isaiah saw that one day the light would overcome the darkness.

The world is still dark with ignorance, hatred, and death. We
know that children starve, terrorists strike, and armies retaliate against

the innocent. Hard workers lose their jobs, sick people die, and drunk drivers commit murder. Preschoolers are abused, women are molested, and senior citizens are mistreated. Wealthy people find it hard to give, lonely people do not find the friends they need, and lost people will not find their way home.

If it is not dark for us this minute, we should be grateful even as we recognize that it will be dark again. The day always turns into night. The dark shadows never go away completely. Not all our dreams will come true. We will not always love our jobs. Our families will have problems we never imagined. Someone will leave too soon, and we will pray for a sunny day. When life seems hard, we need to remember that no matter how dark it gets, a flickering light tickles the retina just enough to give us hope.

Some of the places we go are shadowy. Some of the people we know have not seen any light in a long time. We become the lights in our homes, neighborhoods, schools, workplaces, and churches. God's light illumines everything we do. We become candles that keep others from cursing the darkness, candles on birthday cakes that celebrate life, flashlights that make emergencies less terrifying, searchlights looking for those who have lost their way, lighthouses leading sinking ships to shore, and traffic lights pointing out when to stop.

Our greatest joy comes in shining our little light. Light is the joy of a doctor giving sight to the blind, a lawyer protecting someone who is innocent, and a follower of Christ brightening an area where there was only darkness. Joy comes in being what we are meant to be, doing what we are meant to do, and shining as we are meant to shine.

Joy is the light and hope that we eat and drink at the table. This child of light, whose birthday Isaiah dreamed about, took on the darkness so that we could see the light. We cannot prove it, but if we look carefully, we may see a flicker of hope.

Baptism Isn't for Cowards

Luke 3:15-22

When Jesus also had been baptized and was praying, the heaven was opened, and the Holy Spirit descended upon him in bodily form like a dove. And a voice came from heaven, "You are my Son, the Beloved; with you I am well pleased." (Luke 3:21-22)

The most skeptical New Testament scholars, the ones who question the historicity of almost everything, agree on this story. The baptism of Jesus happened as certainly as any event in the Gospels. Scholars come to this conclusion not only because three Gospels record it but also because the early church wouldn't have told this story if they didn't have to. Jesus' baptism is embarrassing and hard to explain. Why would the child of God submit to a baptism of repentance? If baptism symbolizes the forgiveness of sins and Jesus is sinless, then what does Jesus' baptism mean?

Matthew points out that John himself was uneasy. Mark hurries past the baptism in only three verses. Luke makes as little of the event as possible, casually mentioning that Jesus was baptized *after* mentioning that John is in prison. Jesus' baptism, not unlike our own, is hard to understand.

This story is difficult, in part, because John the Baptist is difficult. John storms out of the wilderness proclaiming a new kingdom, coming in water and fire, and warning especially the religious people of the approaching wrath. John's baptism is revolutionary. He treats

Jews like Jews treated pagan converts, requiring them to be baptized, calling them to repentance.

Surprisingly, crowds flock to John to be baptized, but John does not allow his popularity to detract from his mission. He knows that his work is preparatory. After him, one will come who will baptize not in water but in Spirit.

The day comes when that one wades out into the muddy Jordan. When Jesus comes up out of the water, he sees heaven split wide open and the Spirit descending like a dove. He hears the voice of God saying, "This is my child."

The people gathered on the shore have no idea what it means. They assume that Jesus is now one of John's disciples. Without the rest of Jesus' life, his baptism is incomprehensible.

The purpose of Jesus' baptism is seen in the days and years that follow that afternoon in the Jordan. When we see Jesus take his place with hurting people, his baptism starts to make sense. Jesus' baptism in the Jordan foreshadows his baptism on the cross. Baptism in the river is Jesus' commissioning for ministry.

During the week before Jesus' death, the leaders of the temple challenge him, "By what authority do you do these things?"

Jesus answers with a reference to his baptism: "Was the baptism of John from heaven or not? I was baptized. That's how all this started."

In the waters of baptism, Jesus hears the Spirit calling him to speak the truth and live with grace. Jesus was true to the voice. He gave everything—his days and nights, his hopes and dreams, his work and his life. Jesus gave himself to God's people—sharing, listening, and ministering. When Jesus cried on the cross, "It is finished," it was his baptism that was complete.

Baptisms, like most beginnings, find their meaning after the event. Starting, by itself, is of little consequence. Beginning is easy. Finishing is hard.

Bobby Knight, a Hall of Fame basketball coach who is seldom quoted in books on the Lord's Supper, was asked about a player who was doing a great job coming off the bench. "When will he get to start?" the person wondered.

Coach Knight responded, "You don't understand the game. It doesn't matter who starts. It matters who finishes."

The significance of any decision takes a while. The first draft does not look like the final copy. The moments of initiation take on meaning when we are true to the promise of that beginning. Some of the people who think they need a new job should fulfill the promise of their old job. We may not need new starts. We may need to fulfill the old ones.

Baptism is the introduction to a book waiting to be written. Beginnings by themselves lack meaning. Our baptisms wait for fulfillment.

Every once in a while, someone asks to be re-baptized. They say something like, "I was sincere when I was baptized. I thought I knew what it meant, but I didn't act like it."

Most of the time, the best response is, "The problem is not with your baptism. Your beginning was fine. You need to live out what you've already started."

Finishing our baptism takes our whole lives. Our days are commentaries on our baptisms. Repentance, conversion, and growth are a lifelong process. Just as Jesus' life gave meaning to his baptism, so our baptisms wait to be given meaning.

When Martin Luther was tempted to give up on following Christ, he would sit in his study and recite as a mantra, "I am baptized. I am baptized. I am baptized."

What did it mean when you were baptized? You might find it helpful to remember what you thought, felt, and did on that day, but the meaning of your baptism is more likely to be seen in what you think, feel, and do this day. Are you grateful for the grace of God? What have you done lately that you would not have done had you not been baptized? We are always answering the question, "Why was I baptized?"

The baptistery and the table are promises of what has begun and what will be. We come to the supper to remember our baptisms and move toward the completion of what God is doing in us. We come to the table to remember that our faith stories are still being written.

EXPLORING

JOHN 1:29-39

When Jesus turned and saw them following, he said to them, "What are you looking for?" They said to him, "Rabbi" (which translated means Teacher), "where are you staying?" He said to them, "Come and see." (John 1:38-39)

The high school senior's alarm goes off way too early. She is used to ignoring it. Her mother starts her imitation of the alarm, which is harder to ignore. She pleads, "Five more minutes, Mom."

Mom bellows, "You don't have five minutes," but the senior knows that she does.

If she skips the milk and puts her Fruit Loops in a plastic bag, she can eat in the car.

The bathroom mirror is irritating. Her hair looks like she slept on it while wearing a hat and being electrocuted. She sprinkles water on her head and hopes for the best.

She is almost awake when she gets to chemistry, which is super frustrating. For some unknown reason, chemistry has rules, but 90 percent of the rules are broken 90 percent of the time, and the teacher says, "This is one of those odd cases; just memorize it." The exceptions to the rules make up the rules, and the rules are wrong more than they are right.

English literature is not much of an improvement. Who decided *Pride and Prejudice* is interesting? Mrs. Bennet makes the senior's mother look normal, Keira Knightley is a lot more appealing than Elizabeth, and something is seriously wrong with Mr. Darcy.

Calculus is not the most helpful class. Integrals, derivatives, optimization, and implicit differentiation are not concepts that come in handy often. The teacher drones on and on, sounding like she is speaking a foreign language, which makes it different from her next class, because her Spanish teacher does not speak a foreign language. He is a football coach whose Spanish *might* get him through a visit to Taco Bell.

Her friends want pizza for lunch. She points out that they had pizza yesterday, but apparently, "Let's do something different" is not a persuasive argument. Her friends seldom do anything out of the ordinary. They still tell Chuck Norris jokes years too late.

She is late getting back to European history, but she did not miss anything. For what seems like a century, they have been reviewing the revolutions of the nineteenth century, a period of 100 years that she is relatively certain will not be coming back.

She is glad when school is over. When she gets home, she goes online to the same places she went yesterday—bored.com, stupidvideos.com, killsometime.com. She checks her Twitter, plays a little Candy Crush and then some Zombie Shooter for variety.

There is nothing on television. She is not sure she "gets" Nancy Grace.

When her parents get home, the inquisition begins: "How was your day?" "Who did you eat with?" "What did you learn?" "Did you talk to anyone who's cute?"

The nagging starts. Her parents cannot seem to understand that the more they tell her to do something, the less likely she is to do it in a timely manner. It is a simple rule.

She fears that certain parental phrases will be ringing in her head for the rest of her life: "Pick up your clothes." "Make your bed." "Finish your vegetables." "Don't stay out late."

The lectures fit into two categories: the importance of things of which she already knows the importance, and things that are not important but that her parents inexplicably believe to be important.

Two thousand years ago, it was more this way than not. We forget that Jesus' disciples were younger than they look in stained glass, which adds about twenty years. No one is certain, but the disciples were probably teenagers or close to it.

All the disciples had Jewish mothers. They pleaded with their mothers to sleep five more minutes. They had bad hair days. They got tired of the same old thing for lunch. They faced the same fear of ending up with a dull job.

The most excitement they ever knew began when John the Baptist showed up. John is an alarm clock without a snooze button. He is a wild character shouting that a normal day is not nearly enough, that things have to get better, and he means *now*. John imagines a world of justice and compassion.

John the Baptist is standing with two of his students when Jesus walks by. John says, "That's the one to follow. You know how cocky I can be, but I'm not worthy to tie his sandals."

The disciples start following Jesus, who turns and asks, "What are you looking for?"

They answer nervously, "We thought we'd see where you're staying." In other words, "We don't have anything better to do, so we're wondering what you're doing."

Jesus offers the invitation that will change their lives: "Come and see."

They stay with Jesus all day because he is interesting. They have no idea what they are getting themselves into. They do not know that they will end up leaving behind their nets, homes, and friends. They will change their ideas about almost everything.

The sad truth is that most people are bored. They are tired of measuring their lives by how they are doing in their family's eyes or in the eyes of people doing better than they are or worse than they are. If we are going to have a full life, we need to remember that we are not our bank account or our ambitions or our parents' ambitions.

Stay curious. Listen to the lonely. Feed the hungry. Love and be loved. Find good friends who know how to laugh. Care for children. Make the world less racist, less militaristic, and less materialistic.

Think about the faith you have and the faith you wish you had. Make the church more like Christ. Walk in the way of Jesus.

"Come and see" is the invitation to explore without knowing exactly where we are going, but to know that if we catch a glimpse of God, we will also catch a glimpse of who we can be. Do not waste this one odd and precious life we have been given. Come and see what it means to imagine, hope, and believe.

The table is the invitation to make our lives wonderful. Come and see, eat and drink. Hear God calling us to follow.

STEPS IN THE
RIGHT DIRECTION

MATTHEW 4:12-25

Jesus saw two brothers, Simon, who is called Peter, and Andrew his brother, casting a net into the sea—for they were fishermen. And Jesus said to them, "Follow me, and I will make you fish for people." Immediately they left their nets and followed him. (Matthew 4:18-19)

Crucial moments are not usually marked with caution signs, bright red flags, or even the feeling that we are about to make a big decision. Some of the decisions that matter most slip by without us noticing. Some of the choices that seem small are bigger than the ones that appear big. Because the sacred is present in the ordinary, we cannot be sure that any decision is unimportant. Because life is holy, every day and hour is crucial.

Jesus is working in the carpenter's shop when a customer comes in. "Did you hear what happened to John? You'd think he'd know better than to cross King Herod."

Jesus stops sanding a table long enough to hear the whole story. After the customer leaves, Jesus tells Mary, "It is time to go."

He packs up what he can carry and heads out the door. As he walks to Capernaum, he thinks about the preacher who baptized him. Jesus has picked a bad time to begin a ministry. If John could be arrested for what he said about the king's marriage, what is going to happen when Jesus proclaims a new kingdom?

Jesus is walking beside a lake when he sees two men in a rowboat waiting for unsuspecting fish to wander into their nets. What happens next is hard to believe. Jesus offers them a job with no pay, and they accept: "Come with me and I will make you fish for people."

Why should they follow someone who uses such tortured metaphors? But they leave their boat and nets.

Had the sales pitch been, "Come and make more money selling cell phones than you could ever make fishing," it might have made sense. But the invitation and response in this passage seem unlikely. Four fishermen drop what they are doing and head off to maybe-God-knows-where. They don't know what's coming next, but they know what happened to John the Baptist.

We assume that this is not the disciples' first encounter with Jesus. Surely they knew Jesus before this. But Matthew does not feel any need to explain why they would follow Jesus.

The disciples' instant acceptance of Jesus' peculiar invitation is as dramatic as any moment we will encounter. On occasion, we face big decisions about family, jobs, and faith. We stand at a fork in the road and have to choose. We have moments when we feel like we have to act in a particular way for reasons that we cannot explain. We feel the need to sacrifice something we would rather keep in order to follow. We have taken a few big risks.

But most of the time, our lives are not that dramatic. We don't often drop everything to start a new life. The calling of the disciples is more spectacular than what happens to us most days.

Most of my life is routine. I go to work each morning. I make a list of things to do. I respond to e-mails, attend meetings, write sermons, and prepare classes. I usually have a dozen administrative details. The urgency I feel in what I do is only the urgency of keeping up. Most of it does not feel holy. I give too much attention to too many things at once. My day is filled with pleasant people. I receive more credit than I deserve.

My life is not as adventurous as that of the disciples following Jesus into the unknown. Some women and men live each day in danger because of their faith. Some people do astonishing, heroic works. Maybe someday, we will do something spectacular. For now, most of us feel called to less dramatic discipleship. Most days, we answer God's invitation from within the situations in which we find ourselves.

Maybe Jesus' disciples had days when life did not seem sensational, as they walked up and down Galilee from village to village, through Samaria to Jerusalem and back again. Maybe they had days when they thought things were going slow. On those days, they followed with modest faithfulness.

God calls us every hour of every day. God invites us to be friends with one another, practice kindness, and pray for our daily bread. We live out our faithfulness in worship, work, and study. The routine, everyday ways in which we follow Jesus, the way we read Scripture, welcome strangers, share with the poor, and love the people with whom we live are crucially important.

God is at work in a variety of unspectacular ways. God is present in every way that grace is shared, hope is proclaimed, and healing comes. Love spreads word by word. The bucket fills drop by drop. Wrongs are righted one by one.

If we pay attention, then we will see that even a life as unsurprising as most of us think we live is extraordinary: taking a child to school; hugging someone you love good-bye; eating lunch with a friend; trying to do a decent day's work; talking to a neighbor; reading someone else's story; coming to worship. No event is so commonplace that God is not there. Every moment and every word have possibilities.

Grace comes in unspectacular deeds. The novelist John Updike said, "I will try to work steadily, even shyly, in the spirit of those medieval carvers who so fondly sculpted the undersides of choir seats."

We follow in simple acts. Slowly but surely, our priorities change. On the day they first followed Jesus, the disciples were brash, impulsive, and stubborn. They had to learn day by day how to be the church.

We follow Christ with tiny steps. We grow in faith, not only in memorable, never-to-be-forgotten moments but also in the forgettable moments when we decide to pray instead of turning on the computer, when we choose to do better with the next hour than we did with the last, and when we offer help when we do not have to. We become faithful as we confess a misspent hour, an unnecessary word, or a wasted opportunity. We start to follow over and over. In the bread and cup, God offers us another opportunity to take a step in the direction of Christ.

A WRINKLE IN GOD'S PALM

ISAIAH 40:21-31

It is God who sits above the circle of the earth, and its inhabitants are like grasshoppers; who stretches out the heavens like a curtain, and spreads them like a tent to live in. (Isaiah 40:22)

A man calls the highway department to complain about the condition of the road in front of his house. He calls again and again, repeatedly complaining about the potholes and bumps, but they never do anything. The man calls so many times that finally the highway department says that he has convinced them. They will do something. Instead of coming out and repaving the street, they resolve his complaint another way. They put up a sign that says, "Rough Road Ahead."

Every newborn should be given a sign that says, "Rough Road Ahead." Someone said that we are born naked, wet, and hungry, and then things get worse. Who's got trouble? We got trouble.

Your neighbor has rented his house to college students. From the sounds that begin five minutes after you go to bed, you are guessing that they are not on the Dean's List.

The letter "w" on your keyboard is stuck. You are embarrassed to take it to be fixed, because you think you dropped a fingernail clipping in there.

You step out of the shower, look in the mirror, and realize that time may be a great teacher, but it is a lousy beautician.

Life does not arrange itself for our convenience. We do not get to set up everything in a row and know that it will stay in place. Things fall apart. We have problems.

We have health concerns. Your eyes or ears or legs have been giving you trouble, and you try not to think about what you would do without them. Every day you take your emotional temperature on how you feel about dying.

Your mother is in the nursing home. You find it hard to know how to take care of her when you know that she is frustrated that she cannot do what she once could.

Your job is not what you want, but you cannot think of a good way out.

You want to be married and you are not, or you do not want to be married and you are.

You worry about how depressed you get. Somehow you missed out on most of what you dreamed. Life is a rough road.

Even in those times when everything is going well, we know that there are bad days to come. We know that we are called to be with those who are hurting. We cannot hide from the suffering in the world. The latest war or the next war is never far from our thoughts. Those who die of hunger each day are forgotten, but they should not be. Even when we do not have big problems, we need to care for those who do.

We carry around an emptiness, the deep feeling that somehow not everything is right inside our skin. Part of everyone's inner world is the sense of incompleteness.

Maybe that feeling is itself a word from God. Maybe God speaks most clearly through God's absence. Maybe we know God best through missing God.

The Hebrew people are missing God. They know how hard life can be. They have been forced from their homes into exile. They wonder if they will ever get home. They have begun to believe that God has forgotten them. Where is God when they are so miserable? How can they be cared for by God and depressed at the same time?

The prophet preaches hope in the midst of despair. Isaiah proclaims that God will bring them home: "Have you not known? Have you not heard? Haven't you been paying attention? Haven't you heard the truth all your life? God is beyond, within, and over everything. We are grasshoppers by comparison. Creation is past our comprehension, and yet God encompasses the universe.

"When you compare the eternity of God with the brevity of the puny powers that seem so daunting, the rulers of the earth are plants that last a season, wither, and blow away like dust in the wind. The one who sits above the circle of the earth is unequaled.

"Is there any power to which we can compare God? Look at the night skies. Who do you think made all this? God created the stars and calls them out to their appointed places every night. Though they can hardly be counted, God knows them by name.

"Why do people think that God does not understand what's going on? God's way is always partially hidden, but God has no inconsequential creatures in the universe. We are precious in God's sight.

"God does not come and go. God lasts. God does not grow weary. God gives power to the faint, strengthens the weak, and picks up the exhausted."

The words soar as Isaiah promises that those who wait on God will spread their wings like eagles, run and not be weary, and walk and not faint.

We do not think of ourselves as soaring eagles. We run and get weary. We walk and get weary. Sometimes we do not even move and get weary.

To wait for God is to believe that God is at the end of it all, that though life is a rough road, there is hope at the end. When we are alone, God is with us. When we think we cannot go on, God strengthens us. When our heart is broken, God heals us. When we cannot give any more, God gives. When we cannot love, God loves. When we cannot be kind, God is kind for us.

When someone who has been through too much sadness decides to move forward again, though it would be easier to feel only self-pity, God offers strength.

When two old friends have gone years without speaking and one of them decides to try once more, God offers encouragement.

When someone you love is in trouble hundreds of miles away and there seems to be nothing you can do to help, God helps.

When a parent devastated by the death of a child begins to believe that somehow life will go on, God offers the desire to keep going.

Whenever we find ourselves in hopeless situations, God is hope.

Sometimes nothing is harder than holding on. God gives us the power to keep going and, when we cannot keep going, just to keep enduring. God gives us the strength to overcome and, when we cannot overcome, the strength to keep surviving.

When we are tired, worried about our health, concerned about our parents, or troubled about our job, God is the possibility of life.

When we are overwhelmed and yet somehow remember the goodness of God, we can respond in a couple of ways. We can continue in despair, because we have enough reasons to give up, or we can see that we are in the hands of the God who created us. God has the whole world in hand. In the midst of sorrow, can it be enough for us to live inside a wrinkle in God's palm, grateful to be loved?

The Lord's Supper is like other meals—an opportunity for friendship, love, and nourishment. In this meal, God gives strength. We who are confused are searching for direction. We who are afraid are searching for courage. We who are lonely are searching for love. At the table, we discover that God is searching for us. In the supper, God finds us.

GLIMPSES OF GLORY ✓

MARK 9:2-8

Jesus took with him Peter and James and John and led them up a high mountain apart, by themselves. And Jesus was transfigured before them, with clothes that became dazzling white. (Mark 9:2-3)

In his wonder-filled book, *This Sunrise of Wonder,* Michael Mayne writes to his grandchildren, "If I could have waved a fairy grandfather's wand at your birth and wished upon you just one gift it would not have been beauty or riches or a long life: It would have been the gift of wonder." He suggests that they set their sights not on success but on awe. That is what is going on at the Mount of Transfiguration. In this glimpse of glory, God gives the disciples the gift of wonder.

The end is drawing near when Jesus takes his closest friends with him to pray. Peter, James, and John think Jesus is going to share some great secret with them.

With their powers of concentration at the usual level, the disciples are, according to Luke's version of this story, able to doze off. The sound of voices and the brightness of the light wake them. When their eyes are open, they see Jesus' face and clothes shining. Moses and Elijah are there. The disciples are so overwhelmed that they do not ask how they are able to recognize Moses and Elijah. They have never seen a photograph.

This mountaintop experience is an important stop on a hard journey. Jesus is frustrated that the disciples are not turning out to be all that he hoped. We, too, are disappointed when we realize that the people who want to spend time with us are not the shiniest Krispy

Kremes in the box. Even in the company of his closest friends, Jesus feels alone. Maybe Moses and Elijah are there because there is not a soul on earth who really understands. But these two know what it is like to be alone. They lived with ungrateful, misunderstanding people.

A popular Jewish expectation was that leaders from Israel's past would reappear at the coming of the kingdom. The presence of Moses and Elijah is a sign of God's approval. When the disciples see what is happening, they are overcome. Peter's comment, "Let's make three houses," is peculiar, but he does not want this moment to end. Mark excuses Peter's suggestion by stating the obvious: Peter does not know what to say.

A cloud envelops them, and from the cloud they hear a voice: "This is my dear child; do what he tells you." In other words, "Be quiet. Listen. Pay attention."

The voice instructs disciples to listen, pay attention, and catch a glimpse of glory. Linguistic scholars believe the root "lig" in the word "religion" means "to pay attention" or "to give care." A truly religious attitude is carefully paying attention as part of the process of learning to be grateful. At the back of our brains, there is a too-often forgotten sense of astonishment.

In Charles Schultz's *Charlie Brown*, Snoopy's brother Spike, who lives in the desert, is sitting with his back against a cactus, writing a letter: "At night the sun goes down, and the stars come out; and then in the morning the sun comes up again. It's so exciting to live in the desert."

We have gotten used to sunrises and sunsets, mornings and evenings, the moon and the stars. We have gotten used to music and art, friends and family, joy and sorrow. We easily grow accustomed to the wonders that surround us. Laziness keeps us from seeing the flashes of brightness.

Passing through our one and only earthly life and missing its glories is a disaster. We need to see the depths of beauty. We do not need to turn away from ugly facts. Dreariness, tragedy, and war are real, but no more real than hope, joy, and peace. If we live with a heightened perception of reality, then we will discover the springs of wonder that are just beneath the surface. We need a sense of awe, or we will miss what is most real. The world is filled with intimations of the divine.

For most of us, there have been moments when a word was spoken and we heard more than a word. We have seen more than we let on. We have felt more than we describe. By a certain combination of words on a page, by the way paint is placed on a canvas or notes on a score, we have been moved, because those words, colors, and music speak of something beyond. Some moments transcend time and space and speak to our hearts. We have, from time to time, felt the grace of God.

We sense the holy in the distant stars, in the sudden brilliance of a tree that has been in our backyard for years, and in what happens to a cup of coffee when the cream goes in. The world is sacramental. Creation is marked with the signature of its Creator. The way to the holy is through the ordinary.

People have been transformed by reading a single poem by Wordsworth, listening to a symphony by Mozart, or seeing a painting by Monet. For some of us, it is less often Wordsworth than Anna Quindlen, less often Mozart than Adele, less often Monet than Dilbert. We keep looking for what exalts our spirits, opens our eyes, and makes us better.

Saul Bellow asked, "What if some genius was to do with common life what Einstein did with matter? Finding its energies, uncovering its radiance."

We are capable of more than we realize. Every day is an opportunity. If we will open our eyes, we will find that moments of God's presence lie like unopened gifts at every turn of the road. As we exercise our sense of wonder, we realize that the God beyond us is in our midst.

Our everyday life is not every day. The surface of what we see and hear is not all there is. When you laugh, when you cry, when you feel hope, open yourself to the possibilities. The potential that God has placed within us is breathtaking. Christ calls his disciples to catch a glimpse of glory and live with awe. In the bread of life, Christ invites his disciples out of the sleep of death into the light of wonder. Open your eyes. Listen carefully. Pay attention.

Lent

Praying Desperately

Hear, O LORD, when I cry aloud,
be gracious to me and answer me!
"Come," my heart says, "seek God's face!"
Your face, LORD, do I seek.
Do not hide your face from me. (Psalm 27:7-9)

Most hymnals include a topical index that lists lots of songs of praise and adoration. When we come to worship feeling fine, we have dozens of songs from which to choose. It's different when life is falling apart. While there are many songs on joy, there are only a few listed under "sorrow." If there is a heading for affliction and tribulation, only a few songs fall under it. We see lots of hymns on encouragement but not many on discouragement. Our hymnals need a section for the blues.

In "Hard Times," Ray Charles sings,

My mother told me
Before she passed away
Said son when I'm gone
Don't forget to pray
'Cause there'll be hard times
Who knows better than I?
...
Yeah Lord, yeah, one of these days
There'll be no more sorrow
When I pass away
And no more hard times

I said no more hard times.
Yeah Lord, who knows better than I?

There aren't nearly enough Ray Charles songs in our hymnals. And who hasn't felt like singing this line from W. C. Handy's "St. Louis Blues"? "If I feel tomorrow, like I feel today, I'm gonna pack my trunk and make my getaway."

Everyone has had the urge to pack a trunk. In our lowest moments, we understand The Marshall Tucker Band's "Can't You See?"

> I'm gonna take a freight train,
> down at the station, Lord
> And I don't care where it goes
> Gonna climb a mountain,
> the highest mountain, Lord
> And jump off,
> nobody gonna know
> …
> I'm gonna find me a hole in the wall,
> I'm gonna crawl inside and die.

We need a blues section in our hymnals, because we know what it means to feel blue. We want to get away. We want to crawl inside a hole in the wall. We have burdens that we cannot carry. When we come to church feeling broken, we ought to be able to sing the blues.

Psalms has a blues section. Almost every psalm was written for worship. If Psalms had a topical index, the largest heading would be "Laments." In fifty-two psalms, worshipers cry out to God, scream for help, and pray for deliverance. The Bible encourages us to let God know how hard life is.

Psalm 27 is two psalms put together. Verses 1-6 are a happy song that once stood alone but ended up combined with the lament in verses 7-14 to make the sad psalm easier to sing. This is a blues song:

God, I'm crying to you.
I need your help.
I want your help.
I'm begging for help.
Don't hide from me, God.
I need you, because you're the only who can save me.
My mother and my father have given up on me.
But you can't, God.
Everybody is against me, but don't let them win.
Don't let me fall apart.
I need your help.
I want your help.
I'm begging for help.

Psalm 27 should be read with a wailing harmonica in the background. When we are hurting, we need to pray the blues.

Henry David Thoreau said, "The mass of men lead lives of quiet desperation." But we are not supposed to be quiet about our desperation. We are supposed to pray about it.

The Sunday school teacher got in late on Saturday night, so she doesn't have much of a lesson prepared. She hopes the prayer concerns will take a while. She begins, "I'm excited about our lesson on Psalm 27. I don't think it's going to replace Psalm 23 as anyone's favorite, but it's interesting. Before we turn to the text, what prayer concerns do you have?"

The class responds as they do each Sunday.

"My cousin is having an operation on his left pinky finger. I know it doesn't sound like much, but he says it really hurts."

"My chiropractor is having some back trouble."

"I'm not sure what it is, but my friend said her husband's halitosis is getting worse."

"Be in prayer for my daughter. She's trying to find the right school for my granddaughter—who is a genius. Getting into the right preschool is so important."

"My husband has just gotten a big promotion. It's a lot more money, but it's also a great deal of responsibility for such a young man, so pray for us."

"We won't be at church next Sunday, because my son is in a big karate competition. We're praying that he gets his fuchsia belt."

Then, in the middle of news items masquerading as prayer concerns, someone says something that doesn't fit.

"Six months ago, I took painkillers after my surgery. I haven't been able to stop taking them. I don't want to stop, but I need to pray to stop."

The room becomes quiet. No one is sure how to respond. A woman who seldom speaks says, "My husband died five years ago, and people don't talk to me about him anymore. I've started to forget things about him that I used to know, and it makes me cry. You're not supposed to be crying five years after someone dies."

More silence, and then a father speaks.

"I'm always talking about how well my son is doing. This week he got drunk and wrecked his car. Now I realize he's had a drinking problem for some time. I don't know how to make him understand how serious this is."

The woman seated next to him says, "Thank you for saying what you're really praying for and not just what sounds like a normal prayer request. I've been thinking about prayer this week and I've decided I've been missing a lot. I'm always praying for my sick friends, my family, and my problems. That can't be enough. Shouldn't we pray about the problems in the world?"

The teacher is taken aback at her class becoming an episode of *Desperate Prayer Lives.* She asks a question that is not in her notes: "What should we be praying about?" And the people respond.

"We need to pray for the earth. We're not leaving it in good shape for our grandchildren."

"We need to pray for Christians around the world. The church is too timid."

"We need to pray for people who are lonely. It's hard to be by yourself."

"We need to pray about hunger. When I hear the statistics— 25,000 a day dying—the numbers are so overwhelming that I don't want to believe it's true, because then I'd have to do something."

"I've stopped praying about wars. I can't keep straight who's killing who, but I should keep praying about it."

We are not used to praying about the fear that fills the world. Though it may be more than we can imagine, it is not more than we can pray about.

On the night before he is to die, Jesus gathers his closest friends for a last meal together. Pretending everything is going to be okay would be easier, but it would not be true. Jesus tells them that he is going to die a horrible death. He is going to die for the sorrows in the world. He takes bread and a cup and prays, sharing his broken heart with God. We come to the table because we, too, need to ask God for help.

THE WIND AND THE SPIRIT

JOHN 3:1-10

Nicodemus said to him, "How can these things be?" Jesus answered him, "Are you a teacher of Israel, and yet you do not understand these things?" (John 3:9-10)

What would you do differently if you could start over? What would you change if you could be born again? If I could edit my life, I would skip junior high football, wrecking my father's car, and the last five minutes of my first date. I would stop my mother throwing away my baseball cards. I would go to Baylor again, but I would skip astronomy and take philosophy, even though I heard it was hard. I would not watch *The Beverly Hillbillies*. Well, I might watch one episode because that would be enough to get the main idea. I would read more Mark Twain and less Ann Landers, listen to more Louis Armstrong, and save the six dollars I spent on a Bee Gees album.

Every once in a while, we realize that our lives could be different, and we make plans to turn over a new leaf. We list everything that will not be part of our new life and everything we will start doing more of—exercising, reading great books, spending time with the people we love. Our new plan works for a while.

We also have moments when we realize that, even if we could stop doing everything wrong that we want to stop doing wrong and do everything right that we want to do right—even if we kept the rules that we make for ourselves—there would still be something missing.

Nicodemus visits Jesus because something is missing. He knows that there has to be more. Nicodemus is a good person who does not do the things you are not supposed to do; he does the things you are supposed to do. He is chair of the religion department at the university and a mover and shaker in the ministerial association. He has a column in the local paper. Being a professional expert on God is good work if you can get it. Nicodemus is adept at articulating the intricacies of religion and detecting the logical shortcomings in other people's faith.

Most of us recognize Nicodemus. We have treated our opinions as if they were God's. Sometimes we speak about God as if God is no harder to understand than anyone else. We have held some beliefs for so long that if they aren't God's, we think they ought to be. We begin to believe that if we don't know something, then it doesn't matter. We share Nicodemus's ability to judge what others think on the basis of how close it is to what we think.

Nicodemus coming to see Jesus is surprising. As far as the ministerial association is concerned, Jesus is a nobody. His only status with the local clergy is as a pain in the neck. Just that week, he overturned tables during a big stewardship campaign at the temple.

Nicodemus knows that he cannot explain his desire to see Jesus, so he decides that, with his own status to uphold, it might be smart to pay his visit at night. As a result of his decision, many preachers have been unable to resist the temptation to title sermons on this passage "Nic at Night."

Jesus and the disciples are sitting in an olive grove after a busy day and a long walk. They have finished dinner—fish again—when they hear Nicodemus making his way up the hill, twigs snapping under his feet. Jesus has a puzzled look on his face.

Nicodemus is uncomfortable being there so late at night. Jesus gestures for him to go ahead. Nicodemus begins, as debaters often do, with a compliment: "Jesus, we know that you are a remarkable person with rare gifts for teaching. You do extraordinary things."

He is having trouble getting to what he wants to say. Jesus thinks it is too late for long, drawn-out analysis, so he cuts to the chase. "What the whole thing boils down to is that unless you are born from above, you might as well give up."

Nicodemus was expecting a different response. "I came here for a serious conversation at considerable risk to my reputation, and you speak in riddles. What do you mean? How are you supposed to be born again when you're pushing sixty-five? How can you be born from above when it's a challenge just to get out of bed in the morning?"

Jesus explains, "The wind blows where it will, and you hear it, but you don't know where it comes from or where it goes. That's how it is with everyone who's born of the Spirit."

Jesus is playing on the word *pneuma*, which means both spirit and wind. God's Spirit is as uncontrollable as the wind. The new life that Jesus has in mind is elusive, mysterious, and entirely God's doing.

Nicodemus's last words to Jesus make him the patron saint for all of us who are not sure how to begin anything we are not in charge of: "How can this be?"

Jesus sounds surprised. "You're a teacher, and you don't understand this."

To paraphrase Frederick Buechner from *Peculiar Treasures*, maybe Nicodemus has multiple doctorates, a half column in *Who's Who*, and the ability to theologize with the best, but if he does not understand that life is God's gift, then he'd better start all over again. Nothing is more basic than understanding that God is a wind beyond our understanding. None of us are experts on the Almighty.

The incomprehensible wind of the Spirit blows in places we have not seen. More people know the grace of God than we recognize. We experience God's grace in more ways than we understand.

The new life that God brings is not about knowledge or accomplishment. Being born from above is not the same thing as being a nicer person, learning more, or working harder. We cannot give ourselves a new start. If everyone in the world read the Bible, joined a church, and said hello to their neighbors, something would still be missing.

We need more than the finest blueprint we can design. We need something that transcends what we think of as starting over. We need to be open to God's Spirit, celebrate God's presence, and listen for God's leading. We cannot control when we will feel God's Spirit, but we can live with hopeful expectancy. The winds of grace will transform our values, change our perspectives, and help us see beyond the world's standards.

We can take the dangerous path of worshiping God, following Christ, pouring ourselves out, dying to self-serving ways, and being reborn in the life of the Spirit.

The Gospel of John does not tell us what Nicodemus felt as he left Jesus that night, but after Jesus died, Nicodemus came to the cross and cared for Jesus' body. Nicodemus did not understand God, but somehow God's Spirit led him there. The Spirit leads us to Christ's table. We leave our old selves and are reborn.

LIVING WATER

JOHN 4:1-42

A Samaritan woman came to draw water, and Jesus said to her, "Give me a drink." (The disciples had gone to the city to buy food.) The Samaritan woman said to Jesus, "How is it that you, a Jew, ask a drink of me, a woman of Samaria?" (John 4:7-9)

The high school sophomore wishes the floor would open up and swallow him. He digs his tennis shoes into the rug. The assistant principal is talking to his mother on the phone: "Your son was caught cheating on an algebra exam." This will be a big deal to his parents. Though he tries to convince himself otherwise, it feels like a big deal to him, too. He has been a real jerk this time.

She started coming to worship when everything fell apart. She slips in late, after the greeting, so she will not have to shake hands. She sits near the back and leaves without speaking to anyone. She has trouble with depression, work, and relationships. She thinks that she has more problems than anyone she knows.

He has been going to church all his life. His parents were Sunday school teachers for years. He never went through any teenage rebellion—no drugs, no arrests, no real problems. By Sunday school standards, he is perfect, but he feels like a phony. He is not who people think he is. He does not love others like he knows he should. He looks down on people without any good reasons.

She goes to the well when no one is there. She does not like being ignored by women less than ten feet away. At noon, the well is usually deserted. She walks slowly with a yoke across her shoulders. A bucket hangs from each end. When her steps are not perfect, the wood cuts into the flesh along the back of her neck. From time to time she stops to shift the weight from one bruise to another.

As she straightens up, she sees a man sitting at the well. He appears to be waiting for her. She thinks of turning and running for the village. If he wants to, he can catch her. She curses. Maybe he will just insult her and walk away.

Jesus talks to this woman longer than he talks to anyone else in the Gospels—longer than he talks to any of the disciples, any of the accusers, or anyone in his family.

She is a surprising choice for a long conversation, because she is an outsider—a half-breed, full-blooded pagan as far as the Jews are concerned.

She is also a woman. Women are not allowed to talk in public or worship with men, whose morning devotions include the prayer, "Thank you, God, that I'm not a woman."

She is a Samaritan woman, and she has a reputation. In her younger days, she made Miley Cyrus look like the poster girl for "True Love Waits."

When Jesus lifts his head and asks for a drink, she sees his olive skin and dark eyes. What is a Jew doing here? Has he lost his way? Has he lost his faith?

The Jews have rules about what they can eat and drink. If he drinks water from a Samaritan bucket, he will be breaking the law. But he talks to her as though she matters, as if her being there at the hottest part of the day is not out of the ordinary.

"Could I have a drink of water?" sounds like a simple request.

"But how is it that you, a Jew, ask a drink of me, a Samaritan woman?"

How is it that you, who live in a ritzy neighborhood, ask a drink of me, who lives in subsidized housing? How is it that you, a churchgoer, ask a drink of me, a bartender? How is that you, one of those people who lump everyone who is not like you into one big invisible group, now suddenly ask something of one of us?

While they are not exactly on the same wavelength, the woman understands that she wants whatever Jesus is offering.

"Give me this water" so that I never have to face the women at this well again. "Give me this water" so that I can stay at home and pretend everything is fine.

Jesus startles her by asking about her husband. She could have objected: "That's a little personal. I thought we were talking about religion." She could lie. Instead, she looks him in the eye and says, "I'm not married." With that shred of truth, Jesus tells her more truth about herself. If he knows about her husbands, there is no telling what else he knows, and she would rather not find out. She tries to change the subject back to religion.

"Where should we worship God? At the Samaritans' mountain or the Jewish temple?"

The people who debate the proper ways to worship would not lower themselves to discuss it with this woman, but Jesus talks to her.

Finally, not knowing what else to say, she remarks, "Won't it be great when the Messiah comes? I know that someday hope will win out over despair."

Jesus says, "That time has come."

All this happens at a well that the woman visits every day. This is like having the biggest moment of your life at a convenience store.

The author of John's Gospel includes this story because there is an outsider inside of us. We are not what we should be and not what we wish we were. God loves us anyway. We have done things that are wrong that we have not been able to forget. God loves us anyway. We have scars so deep we think we are the only ones who know about them. God loves us anyway. We do not love others like we should. God loves us anyway. We are not who people think we are. God loves us anyway.

Celie and Shug have a long talk about God. Celie has been abused by life. She tried to be a good Christian for a long time, but now she has given up and decided that God is dead. She describes her gifts from God as "a lynched daddy, a crazy mama, a lowdown dog of a step pa, and a sister I probably won't ever see again."

Shug tries to help Celie believe in God again. Celie finds this astonishing since Shug has never been a churchgoer and has always been what Celie thinks of as a big sinner.

Shug asks Celie to describe the God that she does not believe in: "He big and old and tall and greybearded and white."

Shug replies, "If you wait to find God in the white folks' church that's the one who is bound to show up. When I found out God was white, and a man, I lost interest."

In *The Color Purple*, Shug is the Samaritan woman. Prejudiced people keep telling her that God does not care for her. But like the Samaritan woman, Shug hears a new voice:

> Here's the thing I believe . . . . You come into the world with God. But only them that search for it inside find it . . . . My first step away from [God as] the old white man was trees. Then air. Then birds. Then other people. . . . God love everything you love and a mess of stuff you don't. . . . When you know God loves 'em you enjoys 'em a lot more. You can just relax . . . and praise God by liking what you like. . . . People think pleasing God is all God care about. But any fool living in the world can see [God] always trying to please us back. (Alice Walker, *The Color Purple* [New York: Pocket, 1982] 199–204)

The Samaritan woman runs home to her neighbors. She sounds like there is a fountain springing up inside her. She is in such a hurry that she leaves her water jar at the well.

God invites us to leave behind the "should haves," "ought tos," and "never wills." God wants us to leave behind the times we let God down. God wants us to let go of our insecurities, apathy, and fears.

God who knows us best says, "All that you are, even the secret parts you don't think anyone knows about, are forgiven. No matter what you've done or will do, you're invited to know and love me, and to be known and loved by me."

The waters of God's grace are for anyone who needs a drink. The cup at the table is filled at the spring of living water.

THE PROPOSAL

ISAIAH 55:1-71

Ho, everyone who thirsts, come to the waters; and you that have no money, come, buy and eat! Come, buy wine and milk without money and without price. (Isaiah 55:1)

When I go to the first baseball game of the season, as the first vendor makes his way up the aisle, I will think of John Hunter. John must be in his sixties by now. The last time I saw him, he was working for the Fort Worth Cats—a minor league team. His specialties are hot dogs and making people smile. He is not what we expect of vendors. He walks slowly up and down the aisles, shouting in a way that is hard to describe. He yells, "Haaaaaaawt dawgs." That's it. The monotone is unexpected. You get the feeling that if we were selling a gourmet dinner, it would sound the same—"paaaaaaate."

Vendors peddling their products usually focus on the quality of the product: "Hot dogs, get your hot dogs, hot mustard, hot relish, spicy stadium frankfurters, get your scrumptious, mouth-watering delectable dogs, get 'em right here." The best peddlers make a wiener on a bun sound like a seven-course meal. The hot dog itself is often disappointing.

The vendor in Isaiah 55 has a product that lives up to its billing. The song begins with a street corner vendor shouting, "Ho," for which we may need a new translation, but for them it was the ancient equivalent of "get 'em right here." With running water as close as the nearest faucet, we do not need water vendors, but in Palestine, water was precious and expensive, a commodity bought and sold in the street.

But this vendor is not *selling* water. God is giving it away: "Come, everyone who's thirsty—here's water! Come you that have no money—buy grain and eat! Come! Buy wine and milk—it costs you nothing! Come! Drink your fill! It's free!

Those who heard were astounded. No grocery store ever used this slogan in their newspaper ad: "You who have no money, come get wine and milk—no charge."

We have gotten phone calls that begin, "Hi. We'd like to give you a subscription to *Time, Sports Illustrated,* or *Christianity Yesterday.*"

We respond, "Thank you. I'm not interested."

"We'd like to send you on an all-expenses-paid trip to the Bahamas."

"Thank you. I'm not interested."

"We'd like to give you a year's supply of hot dogs."

"Thank you. I'm not interested."

We know that nothing is free. We may like *Time* and the Bahamas, and sometimes a hot dog hits the spot, but if we need it, we will get it for ourselves.

That is what makes it hard for us to accept that our deepest need is one that we cannot take care of on our own. This hymn in Isaiah is for people who are hungry and thirsty for joy and hope, who are tired and need rest, who are not satisfied with their lives, and who recognize that they need something that they cannot create.

The Israelites were missing something important. They were a conquered nation in exile. Their enemies destroyed the temple. They were far from home, living with strange people with peculiar beliefs. Something was definitely missing.

We do not want to confess the emptiness we feel, to admit that, left to our own devices, we find that our own devices are not enough. We work for the promotion that promises success. We look for the spouse who will make everything right. We plan to lose ten pounds and walk every day. We fill our schedules with "quadrant two" time management activities, but at the end of the day it is not what we have dreamed. We wait in line to drink from the fountain, but we come away with parched throats. We hunger to be loved.

The Israelites had to decide what to do with their deepest longings. They had been in captivity for fifty years, but the Babylonians treated them well. They allowed them to buy property and engage in business. The Israelites had been successful. King Cyrus told them they could go home. He knew they would not. They did not want to leave what they had gotten used to. They did not miss the home they had never known. Though the king said they were free to go, they were captive to a way of life. They knew that they were not really at home, but they had given up on ever really being at home anywhere.

We keep working for the day when we feel completely at home, but we recognize that the fulfillment we can create is temporary at best. Some of the people who have the job we think will make us complete, the family that is almost perfect, the success we want, and the life we want are empty inside. The Israelites sang, "Why do we spend money for what is not bread, and wages for what does not satisfy? Why do we work for what doesn't matter?"

Most of the Israelites decided to stay in Babylon. They would not part with what they had. But a few decided that God's offer was too good to refuse. They went home and rebuilt the temple and sang this hymn, giving thanks for God's grace.

Mrs. Watts, an elderly widow, recognizes that she will die soon. She lives with her son and daughter-in-law in a small apartment in Houston in Horton Foote's *The Trip to Bountiful.* Her heart's desire is to return to her hometown, Bountiful, one more time. She ends up stuck in a bus station twelve miles from Bountiful, waiting for morning to come, hoping that someone will take her the rest of the way. She is happy just to be this close to home:

Why is it that on some days everything goes right, and on other days, nothing goes right? I guess the Lord's just with me today. I wonder why the Lord's not with us every day. Well, maybe then we wouldn't appreciate it so much those days when God is with us. Or maybe, God's with us always, and we just don't know it. Maybe I

had to wait twenty years cooped up in the city before I could
appreciate going home. (Peter Masterson, dir. *The Trip to Bountiful*,
1985)

We long to go home and feel the grace of God. Deep down, we
know that it is when we find our home in God's grace that we will
find peace with who we are. In God's grace, we will learn how to live
in the world that makes us long for home. The Lord is with us every
day. When we are hungry and thirsty, God offers bread and cup. God
gives grace to the ambitious and rest to the weary.

DEATH AND LIFE

JOHN 11:17-44

When he had said this, he cried with a loud voice, "Lazarus, come out!" The dead man came out, his hands and feet bound with strips of cloth, and his face wrapped in a cloth. (John 11:43-44)

I miss Harry O'Dell. Harry played trumpet for the St. Louis Cardinals band. He knew Dizzy Dean, Ducky Medwick, and Stan "The Man" Musial.

I miss Bob Doty. He used to do my taxes without making fun of me for desperately needing someone to do my taxes.

I miss Loyd Turner. Baylor's football team is winning, and Loyd's not here to see it.

I miss Bob Hammond. So does my son. Graham went to Bob's once a month to play chicken foot dominoes.

I miss J. P. Allen. When he was a pastor, he helped the church where I became the pastor start caring for the poor when few Baptist churches even thought about caring for the poor.

I miss Kay Plume. It was a joy to see her with Hank. Hank loves to say, "We went on a honeymoon in 1948 and never came back."

I miss Gene Thompson. I used to call Gene to ask about people I could not place. Gene never forgot a face or a name.

I miss Ed Schmeltekopf. Lots of us lived under the umbrella of Ed's kindness.

I miss Bill Hendricks. Bill said things like, "Brett, I was surprised that you would preach on John 11 without referencing Eugene O'Neill's *Lazarus Laughed.* The play premiered on April 9, 1928, and

closed less than a week later, but I think you might find it helpful."
Neither Bill nor I were surprised that I do not know an obscure
Eugene O'Neill play, but it would be kind of Bill to say it that way.

We lose so many good people.

When Jesus finally arrives at his friends' home, Lazarus has been
dead for four days. Martha wants to hold back her criticism, but she
cannot: "If you had been here, my brother wouldn't have died. You
should've been here."

No sooner are those words out of her mouth than they are
followed by words that defy the facts. "Even yet," she says with
desperate hope, "I know that God will give you whatever you ask."

Jesus replies, "Your brother will live again."

Martha answers that she believes that there is something beyond
the grave.

Jesus speaks for eternity: "You don't have to wait for the end. I
am, right now, resurrection and life. Those who believe in me, even
though they die, will live."

Mary runs up and falls at Jesus' feet, weeping passionately. When
Jesus sees her sobbing, he says, "Where did you put him?"

Jesus breaks down and cries for this family he loves. He orders
them to roll away the stone, and he cries into the cave, "Lazarus, come
out."

The cadaver comes out wrapped from head to toe with a sheet
over his face. Jesus says, "Unwrap him and let him loose."

What would a scientist have seen if one had been there? What
would a poet have seen? The truth of the story is clear to the writer of
the fourth Gospel—God brings life in Christ.

Lazarus Laughed was one of Eugene O'Neill's least popular plays.
The play begins where the story in John leaves off. As the curtain goes
up, Lazarus is stumbling out of the dark, blinking into the sunlight.
After the grave clothes are taken off, he begins to laugh. He hugs Jesus.
He hugs his sisters. He hugs everyone he can get to. He looks as if he
is seeing the world for the first time. He looks up at the sky, the trees,
and the neighbors as if he has never seen them before.

The first words he utters are, "Yes, yes, yes."

He makes his way back to his house, and the whole village of Bethany is amazed. Someone gets the courage to ask what is on everyone's mind. "Lazarus, tell us what it's like to die. What's on the other side of this boundary that none of us have crossed?"

Lazarus begins to laugh even more intensely.

> There is no death, really. There is only life. There is only God. There is only incredible joy. Death is not the way it appears from this side. Death is not an abyss into which we go into chaos. It is, rather, a portal through which we move into everlasting life. The one that meets us there is the same generosity that gave us our lives in the beginning, the one who gave us our birth. Not because we deserved it but because that generous one wanted us to be and therefore there is nothing to fear. The grave is as empty as a doorway is empty. There is nothing to fear. Our great agenda is to learn to accept, to learn to trust. We are put here to learn to love more fully. There is only life. There is no death. (Eugene O'Neill, *Complete Plays 1920-1931*, New York: Library of America, 1988, 537-628)

The communion of saints is made up of those who have learned that there is nothing to fear, those who have learned to trust, and those who have learned to love more fully. They have gone before us in the relay race of faith. This marathon of hope includes the great cloud of witnesses who have moved to the grandstands but are still there to cheer us on as we run our race. They challenge us to be more than we are and become more like the good that was in them. They tell us how far we have to go.

We need to chase after Christ with reckless abandon, even when he leads us to minister in lousy places that good sense tells us not to visit. We follow because Christ is where death ends and life begins. God brings life on both sides of the grave.

Resurrection happens when we overcome our bad habits by the grace of God. Resurrection happens when a church allows itself to be moved by the Spirit into daring ministries. Resurrection happens when a nation is stirred to work toward justice for all its citizens, to see that the hungry are fed and the poor are treated with compassion.

Resurrection happens when we die to our old selves and are born once more to the selves God means for us to be.

When we share Communion, we recognize that Christ's followers are with us. The saints challenge us to live with joy. Be delighted when anyone besides the Yankees wins the World Series. Do not worry about not being able to do your own taxes. Cheer for your team even if they are lousy. Play chicken foot dominoes as though it matters. Care for the poor. Love the people with whom you live. Put names and faces together. Be an umbrella of kindness for someone. Tell a friend about a play they would enjoy. Remember someone you miss.

The Communion table is bigger than it looks. The table goes on forever, back centuries and across continents. We take our place with sisters and brothers who shared the journey of faith and whose lives still inspire, encourage, and challenge us. We pass the bread and cup as part of the family that includes everyone who has found life in Christ. In the supper, God invites us from our tombs of caution into a world of freedom.

Holy Week

TRIUMPH AND TRAGEDY

LUKE 19:28-40

As Jesus was now approaching the path down from the Mount of Olives, the whole multitude of the disciples began to praise God joyfully with a loud voice for all the deeds of power that they had seen, saying, "Blessed is the king who comes in the name of the Lord!" (Luke 19:37-38)

Karol Daniel was my college Sunday school teacher. For graduation, she gave the seniors books she thought we would enjoy. She gave the English major a book of poetry by John Keats and the physics major a biography of Albert Einstein. Jon Stewart had not written anything yet, so she gave me a theology book—Sam Keen's *To a Dancing God.* Shortly after the gift, but before the thank-you note, I read a review by a cantankerous critique who wrote, "The world is too filled with tragedy to do as Mr. Keen suggests and simply dance."

When I next saw Karol Daniel, she asked, "How do you like the book?"

I was still trying to convince people I was smart, and so even though I had not read a single page I said, "The world is too filled with tragedy to do as Mr. Keen suggests and simply dance."

Mrs. Daniel looked disappointed. "Oh, Brett, you're better than that."

I am sure she forgot that brief conversation long ago. If I thought she remembered, I would call and say, "You were right. I was foolish.

I'm trying to be better than that. I'm starting to understand that the world is too filled with tragedy not to dance."

Palm Sunday is a day to dance.

Jesus planned the parade. The prophet Zechariah said that the king of peace would come on a donkey. Jesus tells the disciples to go into the village to get a colt that seems to have been owned by a follower of Jesus. "If anyone says to you, 'Why are you doing this?' just say, 'The Lord needs it.'"

Just like Jesus said, as they are untying the donkey the owner says, "What are you doing?"

"The Lord needs it."

They do not have a saddle, so they throw their coats on the colt. Jesus rides sidesaddle, because if he straddled the donkey his feet would drag the ground.

When Jesus comes over the crest of the Mount of Olives, he sees the road packed like Times Square on New Year's Eve. The cobblestone street is lined with people who know how wonderful a good parade can be, and that this is the best parade ever. Jesus rides like a conquering king into his capital city. The people wave palm branches and throw down their coats.

Throwing your coat before a donkey is like tossing your sports jacket in front of a limo. The coat is going to be significantly worse for wear.

Jesus' followers are ecstatic. They have seen Jesus heal the sick and feed the hungry. They have found such hope in his words that they know he is their long-awaited king. Nothing could keep them from shouting, "Blessed is the one who comes in the name of the Lord. Hosanna in the highest."

They cheer until they are hoarse. They laugh, dance, and sing.

Some people can't stand it when others are having a good time, so the Pharisees say, "Jesus, tell your disciples to calm down."

Jesus knows they are right to cheer. He smiles as he quotes the prophet Habakkuk, "If I did that, the stones in the pavement would have to celebrate in their place."

The disciples think it is the best day ever, and they may be right. What a great crowd. These people know how to celebrate. Jesus is pleased.

We should be pleased, too. We find such hope in Jesus' words. We should cheer until we are hoarse. Nothing should keep us from laughing, dancing, and singing.

We celebrate the hope of a better way, the peace God promises, and the joy of God's grace. We celebrate because we believe, because we need to celebrate, and because triumph and tragedy are closer than most think. Laughter is never far from tears.

Holy Week does not move from one triumph immediately to another, from the parade on Palm Sunday instantly to the celebration on Easter.

On Monday, Jesus clears the temple of those who are there to make a buck.

On Tuesday, Jesus debates the religious scholars who want to arrest him, but the crowd is protecting Jesus.

On Wednesday, Judas Iscariot goes to the authorities and offers to take them to Jesus.

On Thursday, Jesus shares a last supper with his followers. The temple police arrest Jesus.

A group gathers in Pilate's courtyard, but the Palm Sunday crowd is not invited. A few dozen people help the powers get rid of Jesus.

The Palm Sunday crowd consists of those who want to love Jesus, but the Friday crowd considers themselves the protectors of the religious institutions.

Jesus is put to death by a small group of religious people who do not want to change. They do not like what Jesus says about caring for the poor. They do not like the people Jesus runs with. They want to reserve the temple for respectable people, but Jesus thinks everyone should be welcome.

Jesus dies because he feels the blind man's darkness, the cripple's frustration, and the leper's abandonment. Jesus dies because the world is tragic.

Jesus' way of including everyone has not caught on. The powerful still cling to their power. There is always someone we love who is grieving. Poverty tears the world apart. Peace is not as popular as war.

Jerry Falwell, whom I do not often quote, told a group of pastors, "Real ministers never have two good days in a row."

Anyone who follows Christ will find it hard to have two good days in a row—not if you watch the news, not if you love the people God loves.

Dietrich Bonhoeffer wrote,

> The other person is a burden to the Christian, in fact for the Christian most of all. The other person never becomes a burden at all for unbelievers. They simply stay clear of every burden the other person may create for them. Christians, however, must bear the burden of one another. Only as a burden is the other really a brother or sister and not just an object to be controlled. The burden of human beings was even for God so heavy that God had to go to the cross suffering under it. (*Life Together* [New York, Harper and Row, 1954] 100–101)

Palm Sunday lies in the tension between the celebration to which we are called and the sadness that keeps interrupting. Sorrow makes our need for joy clearer.

God invites us to hope that is deeper than our despair. There is too much hunger, too much war, and too much loss not to celebrate.

We celebrate Communion because God is with us through it all. We eat the bread of life in a world filled with death. We drink the cup of joy in a world filled with sadness. We give thanks for God's love and celebrate. Palm Sunday is followed by Good Friday, but then Easter comes.

Betrayals

While they were eating, Jesus said, "Truly I tell you, one of you will betray me." And they became greatly distressed and began to say to him one after another, "Surely not I, Lord?" (Matthew 26:21-22)

The disciples ask one after another, "It's not me, is it, Lord?" Peter, Andrew, James, John: "It's not me, is it, Lord?" Around the table to Judas Iscariot, who softly says, "It's not me, is it, *Rabbi*?"

Judas does not call Jesus "Lord," but "Rabbi." One word puts Judas on the other side of the world.

Jesus replies, "You and I've been together a long time. We've shared a thousand meals. We've eaten out of the same bowl. And yet you betray me." The other disciples are horrified and relieved that it is not them.

Like the eleven, we are glad it is not us. We are not that evil. Judas's behavior is as incomprehensible to us as it was to the disciples. When we watch the news or read the newspaper, we see that there are bad people out there. We are not them. We are not dangerous to anyone. We do not understand how people can do such awful things. We are good people.

In spite of our status as good people, Judas is not as far away as we would like to think. Just as the eleven find safe places to hide when life becomes hard, we know how to disappear. Some days the connection between us and Christ is hard to see.

We are not as loyal as we want to appear. We do not love the Lord our God with all our heart and soul and mind and strength. We do selfish things. We make choices that we know are wrong. We avoid doing some things that we know are right. We have a picture in our heads of what a radical, genuine Christian looks like, and it is not us. Our failures are betrayals.

I find it easier to pray in the morning than in the evening. In the morning, I ask to be aware of God's presence. I think about the things I need to get done and ask God for help. I pray about the day's possibilities. Praying in the morning makes me feel confident that this will be the day when I finally get it together. Morning prayers make me feel better.

Praying in the evening often makes me feel worse. In the evening, I think about the things I have not gotten done. I feel bad about the possibilities that I have missed, the people for whom I have not cared nearly enough. Praying in the evening reminds me that I did not get it together, and so my prayers are filled with confession. Evening prayers are about betrayal.

That is what makes the Lord's Supper so important. What does Jesus do with Judas his betrayer? "Grab him, boys! Let's tie the traitor up and lock him in the basement!" No. Jesus continues the meal. Matthew does not say a word about Judas leaving the table. In this Gospel as in Luke, Jesus includes Judas in the supper. Christ makes a place for his betrayers: "You are my sisters and my brothers. There will always be a place at my table for you."

We come to the holy supper as those who have betrayed Christ and who will betray Christ again. We come to the table only by the grace of God.

"Father, Forgive Them"

Luke 23:32-38

Then Jesus said, "Father, forgive them; for they do not know what they are doing." (Luke 23:34)

When Albert Einstein was about to die, he chose his words carefully and spoke them clearly. He expected his last words to be in the newspaper, become part of his story, and be remembered forever. Unfortunately, Einstein spoke his last words in German, his native tongue, and the nurse who was with him did not speak German.

Lady Nancy Astor spoke her last words when, on her deathbed, she momentarily awoke to find herself surrounded by her entire family: "Am I dying or is this my birthday?"

Oscar Wilde's last words were, "Either that wallpaper goes, or I do."

Some people do not realize it is time for last words. Bing Crosby said, "That was a great game of golf, fellows."

During the Civil War, the last words of General John Sedgwick were, "They couldn't hit an elephant at this distance."

Noel Coward said, "Goodnight my darlings, I'll see you tomorrow." Maybe he knew.

If you only had twenty-five words left, what would you say? What do you believe the most? What would you want to say to those you love whom you will leave behind?

Jesus' last words are hard to hear. The ones who sent Jesus to the cross were well educated. The Roman civilization was the most advanced in the world. The Jewish understanding of God was unparalleled. They accused Jesus of threatening religion and undermining the government. He was guilty of both charges.

Caiaphas the high priest worked hard to keep things running smoothly. He did not need a revolt. A lot of people could die. He was just doing his job. Pilate had nothing personal against Jesus. He wanted to release him, but it would have been more trouble than it was worth. He was just doing his job. Jesus was executed by the church and the state.

They took him to Skull Hill. They threw dice for his clothes. They laughed. "Messiah, that's a good one." They toasted him with sour wine: "To the King of the Jews!"

Jesus responded by praying, "Father, forgive them; they don't know what they're doing."

Those standing around thought it funny to hear a condemned man offering forgiveness. They wondered whom he meant: the Romans, the Jewish leaders, the disciples who disappeared, Caiaphas, Pilate, Judas, the thieves on either side of him?

"Father, forgive them." The form of the Greek verb *elegen* makes it clear that Jesus spoke these words more than once. Jesus *kept* saying, "Father, forgive them."

Ghastly evil and gorgeous good converge in these words. Nailed to a cross, Jesus is still showing God's love. To his dying breath, Jesus keeps harping on forgiveness and loving one's enemies.

We know we need God's forgiveness, so we find some comfort in Jesus' words, but if we listen honestly, there is something in us that is not so sure.

Hearing "Father, forgive them" and nodding our heads in agreement is difficult. We would rather dismiss these words as sweet, admirable, and naïve. If you read the newspaper—terrorists threatening innocent people, fathers molesting their daughters, soldiers killing children—"Father, forgive them" seems outrageous. Do not talk to us about forgiveness until the people who do the hitting have been hit back. Why should we forgive a person who has hurt someone we love? What does it even mean to forgive? Does forgiveness mean condoning abuse? Sometimes talking about forgiveness is a glib way of ignoring evil.

The word "forgiveness" is open to misinterpretation, but the cycle of retaliation is always threatening. Desmond Tutu said, "There is no future without forgiveness."

Sometimes we think that if we set our minds to it, we can *make* ourselves forgive. When psychologists write about how to forgive, they give advice that seems to be helpful. Be honest about your feelings. Do not minimize the pain. Feel your anger and grief. Honestly examine your heart. Ask how you contributed to the situation. Am I angry at behavior that reflects something in me? Accept the fact that the behaviors we condemn in others may be expressions of our own fears.

The problem is that we do not *want* to love people who do not like us. Have you ever tried to forgive someone who has really hurt you? When people hurt us, it is easier to write them off, to make a mental note that we will never be their friend.

We cannot make ourselves forgive, but we can give ourselves to Christ. In giving ourselves to God, we know God's compassion for us and begin to understand God's love for everyone else.

Listen to Jesus pray, "Father, forgive them." When we stand near the cross, discovering that we are loved to the core, we receive not only the forgiveness we need but also the hope of forgiving others. When we realize that we are sinful and forgiven, we have the possibility of offering that same forgiveness to others. When we pray to see others through God's eyes, we slowly begin to see that the other person is as wounded, hurting, and imperfect as we are. This realization sets us free from the need to judge.

Listen to Jesus pray, "Father, forgive them," as we bring before him the people we most fear and despise. Jesus is pleading that God's mercy will be at the center of our lives and theirs.

Jesus' cross-shaped words, "Father, forgive them," are hard to hear, but Christ invites us to eat the bread of forgiveness and drink the cup of grace.

"TODAY YOU WILL BE WITH ME IN PARADISE"

LUKE 23:39-43

Jesus replied, "Truly I tell you, today you will be with me in Paradise." (Luke 23:43)

How do you want to be remembered? What is most important about who you are? What do you want on your tombstone?

The writers of epitaphs try to sum up a life in a few words: "Beloved Mother," "Devoted Husband," "Our Little Angel."

Alexander the Great's epitaph reads, "A tomb now suffices for him for whom the world was not enough." Nothing like being remembered for the size of your ego.

Jefferson Davis's tombstone says, "Defender of the Constitution." Nothing like getting in the last word.

W. C. Fields: "I would rather be living in Philadelphia."

Mel Blanc, the voice of Porky Pig: "That's all, folks."

Al Capone: "My Jesus, Mercy."

John Keats wrote his own epitaph: "Here lies one whose name was writ in water."

Keats's may be the most telling. One of our fears is that we will not be remembered. We will die without a trace and slowly fade from the memories of those who love us, until there will be no one to remember the trace we were. Who will remember us?

There is not one cross, but three. This fact makes the short list of details reported by all four Gospels. Matthew, Mark, Luke, and John make a point of saying that this is a group execution. Jesus is not even given the distinction of solo martyrdom. He is dumped in to make a group of three, a last-minute addition to someone else's execution.

Crucifixion was for common criminals. White-collar criminals from privileged backgrounds with influential connections would never have been crucified. No civic, business, or church leader would have been caught dead on Calvary.

Jesus is keeping the same kind of company he always kept.

According to Matthew and Mark, these two criminals were violent—probably insurrectionists against the Romans, guerillas ambushing a convoy here, hitting an outpost there, killing where they could. The central event in the Bible is God crucified between two terrorists.

Would you in a million years dream of having such an objectionable story at the heart of a faith? Jesus is obscenely displayed, reviled, mocked, spat upon, beaten nearly to death, naked, and covered only with dirt, sweat, blood, and excrement. No such picture of God had been offered in the history of religion.

Jesus is getting most of the attention from the crowd, perhaps because the sign above his head is more spectacular than the others—"This is the King of the Jews." Those on either side are not interesting enough to record.

The first criminal decides to join the crowd in mocking Jesus. Pain and the panic of dying have seized him. Maybe for an instant, some mad hope strikes him that the so-called "Messiah" might pull something off. But he can plainly see that the Messiah is already almost dead. So this murderer spews bitter words at Jesus: "Aren't you the Messiah? I thought you were the Messiah. Everyone says you're the Messiah. Why can't your people get us out of here?"

He doesn't say it under his breath; the criminal way over on the other side of Jesus hears him and tells him to shut up: "Have you no fear of God? You and I are guilty. We earned this. This man did nothing wrong."

No one else in the Gospels ever did what this man does next. He addresses Jesus simply by his name. Others called him Teacher, Rabbi, Master, and Lord. A few said Jesus, Son of David. But in the whole record, no one even once calls him by his simple name.

"Jesus, remember me when you come into your kingdom."

Hanging there bloody, exhausted, and guilty, he still recognizes someone he wants to remember him.

Did he hear Jesus say, "Father, forgive them"? How much did he understand? He understood more than the politicians who were crucifying Jesus. He understood that the kingdom is for prostitutes, tax collectors, lost sheep, wayward children, Samaritans, and penitent thieves.

"Jesus, remember me." This is the prayer of a man who, as death draws near, has seen his wasted life flash before his eyes. He asks only to be remembered kindly.

The answer Jesus gives is far beyond an answer to what the man actually asked. All he asked was to be remembered. Jesus lifts his head and says, "Don't worry. I will. Today you will be with me in Paradise. From now on we're in this together. I won't leave you behind. I'll be with you."

God's presence is Christ's destiny. Jesus will not go to paradise by himself. He will bring with him this one beside him on the cross.

"Jesus, remember me" is the best prayer we can pray.

Our salvation is being made part of God's memory. In the supper, we give ourselves to the one who promises to be with us eternally.

"My God, my God"

Matthew 27:45-49

From noon on, darkness came over the whole land until three in the afternoon. And about three o'clock Jesus cried with a loud voice, "Eli, Eli, lema sabachthani?" that is, "My God, my God, why have you forsaken me?" (Matthew 27:45-46)

Brian of Nazareth has been sentenced to crucifixion. His followers desert him. He is in utter despair, dying on the cross. But at the end of Monty Python's *Life of Brian*, the criminal crucified next to him says, "Cheer up, Brian. You know what they say," and then he sings,

> Some things in life are bad.
> They can really make you mad.
> When you're chewing on life's gristle,
> don't grumble, give a whistle.
> Always look on the bright side of life.
> If life seems jolly rotten, there's something you've forgotten
> and that's to laugh and smile and dance and sing.
> Always look on the bright side of life. (Dir. Terry Jones, written by Terry Jones et al., 1979, HandMade Films)

Soon the whole crowd is singing and whistling.

This absurd scene raises a serious question. Why do Christians act as if faith is meant to make them happy when the central story in the Bible is Jesus' death on the cross? The churches in which I grew up taught me always to look on the bright side of life. They told me that Christians have fewer troubles than other people.

The Jesus I learned about in Sunday school would never have cried, "My God, my God, why have you forsaken me?" Or if he did, he would not mean it. One theory is that in the first century, when the opening verse of a psalm was quoted, it was a reference to the entire psalm. According to this shaky hypothesis, when Jesus called out, "God, why have you forsaken me?" he was referencing a psalm that ends in triumph. Jesus thus meant the opposite of what he said. Jesus was never *really* discouraged.

But that is not how the story reads. Jesus is panting on the cross, dying between two thieves, because he offended the religious people. His promising life is coming to a bloody end. Jesus feels like God has left him. Every joint in his body feels pulled apart. His heart is bursting, and he is dry as a bone. He longs to lie down and let them bury him. Hanging on the cross, deserted by his friends, believing himself abandoned by God, Jesus cries these awful words: "My God, my God, why have you forsaken me?" Jesus pleads for a word from God, but there is not a sound from heaven.

Jesus experiences total abandonment on the cross, for although God is still with him, Jesus does not feel it. The sight of Jesus enduring the worst suffering a human being can know should be the end of any fond hope we might have that following Christ will keep us safe.

Yet this cry of abandonment is also comforting. Jesus understood how heartbreaking God's silence can be. When we wonder where God is, we can know that Jesus wondered, too.

When we read the newspaper, it seems like God has forsaken the world. Suicide bombers take the lives of children. Cars collide. Planes crash. Boats sink. Tornados, hurricanes, and earthquakes destroy. Wars ravage. Children starve.

Life is so hard in many places that it feels like whining to point out that life is hard for all of us. From beginning to end, childhood to retirement, life is difficult. Your parents divorce. You move away from your friends. The bullies never seem to move. When you are in high school, you do not know whether to please your parents or your friends, but you know you cannot please both. People start wanting to know why you are still single long before you should be married. You get tired of eating alone, and when you stay up to watch Conan, your room sounds empty when you laugh out loud. Or you get married. Suddenly you have to explain everything, share everything, and put up with everything. You are always at another's mercy. Maybe you have children. The responsibility is so constant. You are either too strict or too lenient. You get no instruction book and end up second-guessing yourself. You get a job that is not exactly your dream job. Your days have a relentless sameness about them. You are sure that you are not paid nearly enough. You get stuck in resentment. Someone you love gets Alzheimer's. Then you get old. You are tired of reading that Helen Mirren, Diane Keaton, and Goldie Hawn are in their sixties. These women are not representative of what gravity does to normal people. You go to too many funerals for people who were in better shape than you are.

We have days when we wonder what the point is. We pray without any sign that God is listening. We feel abandoned. Sometimes when our longing for God is most intense, God seems most silent. We wonder if God is there . . . or ever has been.

That is where Jesus was from noon to three on Good Friday. He was in the darkness that we know too well. This word from the cross may be the word we most need to hear, because we have known God's absence. We have felt it when someone we love dies, when a dream falls apart, when we see real evil.

Yet even when we feel abandoned, God is with us. All we know is the silence, but the silence is in God. When we feel godforsaken, we feel what Christ felt. At our most hurt, we have one who has been there before and will be with us. If we cry out, "Where are you, God? I feel alone," we do so knowing that Jesus said it first.

Just as there is encouragement in knowing that Jesus went through it too, so there is hope in following Christ's example in the experience of it. Here is the remarkable thing that we have to remember. Even in the deep darkness of feeling godforsaken, Jesus prayed. He still talked to "my God." He felt abandoned. He felt alone. But he kept talking to God.

We will feel alone, but even in the midst of it, we can know that we are not truly alone. When we do not feel God's presence, we can still trust that God is with us in a way that is not dependent on our feelings.

We will have times when it feels like God is absent and silent, but even in that hell, God will hold us. When we are feeling forsaken, we can still pray, "My God, my God."

At the last supper, Jesus gathered his disciples to share his sorrow. We are invited to the table by one who understands our feelings of being abandoned. We come to the supper as Jesus did, knowing that even when we feel forsaken, God is with us.

Easter

EASTER AS THE CHURCH'S STORY

JOHN 20:1-18

Supposing him to be the gardener, she said to him, "Sir, if you have carried him away, tell me where you have laid him, and I will take him away." Jesus said to her, "Mary!" (John 20:15-16)

The thirteenth-century Persian poet Rumi had an interesting way of describing our need for resurrection. He wrote this dialogue:

"The mystics are gathering in the street. Come out!"
"Leave me alone. I'm sick."
"I don't care if you're dead! Jesus is here, and he wants to resurrect somebody!"

What a curious way to put it! "I don't care if you're dead! Jesus is here, and he wants to resurrect somebody!"

Jesus wants to resurrect somebody, but there are good reasons to choose not to be resurrected. The person in Rumi's poem thought he was too sick to be resurrected. Pontius Pilate's desire for power was too great. The Jewish leaders' need to have everyone think like they thought was too high. And for many of us today, the fear of letting go of the routine is a reason not to be resurrected.

Churches have reasons for not being resurrected: "We might offend some of our members." "This isn't how other churches do it." "We've always done it this way." "We've never done it that way."

You may have never been to a church in need of resurrection, but you can imagine one.

In the church in need of resurrection, Sunday school is the same thing every week. The prayer concerns involve sick people. While they definitely need prayer, seldom does anyone mention a war or the crisis in inner-city schools. Most do not talk about their own concerns—the fear of being single, marital problems, a struggle with depression. Few Sunday school attendees have heard a fellow member admit an addiction to alcohol or drugs until he or she is cured.

In the church in need of resurrection, worship is safe. Prayers are predictable. Biblical texts are familiar. Sermons present a timid gospel that avoids whatever issues the congregation and preacher want to avoid. The first time Jesus preached, he told the congregation that they were bigots, and they tried to throw him off a cliff. Three years later, they finally did kill him because they did not like what he preached. Not many preachers tell enough truth to get into this kind of trouble.

In the church in need of resurrection, ministries are cautious. On church websites under the headings "missions" and "ministries," many list the bookstore, the men's breakfast, the women's lunch bunch, the basketball team, and the barbershop quartet. If you go back to Jesus' first sermon, you hear that God anoints Christ and his followers to preach "good news to the poor, release to the captives, sight to the blind, and freedom to the oppressed." Most churches do not spend much time with the poor, blind, or imprisoned.

The church always needs resurrection, but never more so than at the beginning. Early on Easter Sunday morning, the disciples are the world's deadest church.

Mary Magdalene is the first at the cemetery. She goes to the grave of the finest person she has known. She gets there while it's still dark. She isn't sure exactly why she has come. When there is finally enough light for her to see, she feels devastated by what she discovers: "Oh, no, not this. Not only have they beaten him, not only have they murdered him, but now they've stolen his body. How could they do *this?*"

Mary Magdalene has spent most of her life too broken to fix, looking for light in the darkness, more dead than alive. Jesus healed her not from one or two but from *seven* demons. He was her glimmer of hope. Now that he is dead, she has no hope.

With tears in her eyes and fear and anger in her heart, Mary runs from the tomb to tell the disciples what has happened. Peter and John come back to the cemetery with her, but they don't see any reason to hang around, so they go home. Mary stays and cries. What is she waiting for? What does she hope to hear?

Mary watched Jesus die and saw them bury him. He was dead. She stays in the cemetery because she has nowhere else to go. She looks into the tomb and is unimpressed with the angels.

Jesus speaks to her, but she does not recognize him at first: "If you're the gardener, tell me what's happened."

Then Jesus says her name. In a simple word, a single sound, darkness becomes light, despair gives way to hope, and life overcomes death. When Jesus calls her by name, Mary is transformed from the last mourner in a dead church into the first witness of a living church. She has been resurrected.

Mary runs to tell the church to wake up: "I've seen the Lord. I don't care how dead you think you are! Jesus is here, and he wants to resurrect somebody!"

God wants the church to let go of old habits, judgments, and prejudices, stop expecting others to conform to a particular way of doing things, and give up the evil speech that kills congregations.

God will help us stop worrying about whom we might offend and start offering God's grace to everyone. God will teach us not to be limited by what others do but to go where the Spirit leads. God will take us beyond what we have always done and help us carry the best of the past with us as we move forward to a better future.

God will help us pray honestly, fervently, and passionately. God will lead us to open the Bible, ask hard questions, admit our differences, and listen. God is calling the church to new life and demanding ministries. God is inviting us to seek out those who feel almost dead and share God's love with them. God is pleading with us to welcome all kinds of people and become genuine friends. God is calling us to have warm hearts, open minds, and adventurous spirits. At the table, God offers life that overcomes whatever death we have known.

EASTER: THE SEQUELS

MARK 16:1-8

So they went out and fled from the tomb, for terror and amazement had seized them; and they said nothing to anyone, for they were afraid. (Mark 16:8)

The book that you have been waiting for is finally in your mailbox. After you finish supper and put the dishes away, you curl up in your favorite chair and begin to read. Plots develop and intertwine. Characters emerge, evolve, and surprise. Conflicts materialize. Tensions mount. The climax approaches. In the early hours of the morning, you turn the last page expectantly. How will the story end? That question engages, absorbs, and captures us. Whether it is a John Grisham novel, a Harlequin romance, or a Sherlock Holmes mystery, our uncertainty about the conclusion keeps us involved. What could be more frustrating than a story without an ending? What is more disconcerting than a romance in which the secret love is never spoken? A mystery in which the murderer is never identified? A gospel in which the risen Christ is never seen?

On Sunday morning, the men are nowhere to be found. The women stayed at the cross to the bitter end and watched Jesus' burial. They wanted to anoint Jesus on Friday, but everyone was in such a hurry to get the body into the tomb before the Sabbath began that they didn't have a chance. On Saturday evening, they gather the perfumes and oils they will need. Sometimes bad funeral directors give broken-hearted people the impression that spending money is a way to express love. These women may have felt that. Did they bring more spices because it was Jesus?

They are determined to read the last page of the tragedy. The sounds and smells of an early spring morning—the rich odor of the damp earth and birds noisy with anticipation—are wonderful, but the women expect terrible smells and the sound of silence.

They've been so preoccupied with the spices that they don't think about the tombstone until they make their way to it. Gravestones could be a foot thick and six feet in diameter.

The women keep going on this futile errand anyway. Robert Frost said, "The nearest friends can go with anyone to death, comes so far short they might as well not try to go at all." We try nonetheless to nudge the stone just enough to say good-bye.

But the women see that the stone has been pushed out of the way. Their chance to say good-bye has been stolen. They step into the tomb and are startled to see a young man. He says, "Don't be alarmed. Jesus isn't here. Go tell the disciples that he's going ahead of you to Galilee. That's where you'll find him."

Alarmed is exactly what the women are. When they finally stop running, they decide not to say anything to anyone. The whole episode has left them terrified.

That's it.

"They said nothing. They were afraid." And the credits roll. The oldest manuscripts of the Gospel of Mark end with verse 8—"they were afraid." Is that any way to end the story?

The first ones to copy the book of Mark did not like the ending one bit. A century or so later, a longer ending was added. Most modern translations treat the four extra paragraphs like a footnote. Scholars agree that scribes added the additional verses that tell of Jesus' appearance (vv. 9-20) in order to provide a more suitable conclusion.

They have a point. This is not the way a gospel is supposed to end. We read about Jesus calling disciples, telling stories, feeding the hungry, and loving the outcasts. That is followed by opposition, threats, crucifixion, and burial. Then these women at the tomb are alarmed, afraid, and saying nothing to anyone. And that is the end. Why doesn't Mark tell about how Mary recognized Jesus in the garden when he called her name, how Jesus broke bread with two of his followers in Emmaus, or how Thomas finally believed? Finish the story, Mark. Wrap it up. Give us a conclusion.

There is too much unfinished business. Was Jesus waiting for them in Galilee? Did they find him there? How did they find him? What did he say? What did they do? How does the story end?

Instead of the ending of a story, Mark gives us a beginning. He leaves the story hanging at its start. The first verse in the book of Mark is "This is the beginning of the Gospel of Jesus." The whole story is the beginning. In my Bible, Mark is eighteen pages, the length of an introduction. The end of the book is not the end of the Gospel but the end of the prologue.

The angel says, "Jesus is not here; he's risen!" Mark's pen presses hard on one word: "Go." "Go tell the disciples that he's going ahead of you to Galilee; you'll see him there."

Jesus goes on ahead, always out there, beckoning, leading us on, and waiting for us to arrive and discover what is in store for us.

Jesus has risen and left word for them to get going. The disciples are confused and afraid. Mark dramatically puts down his pen, for what happens next remains to be seen. The Easter story has no ending because Easter calls us into the future. The sequels are still being written.

We are invited to go to Galilee to find Jesus. Galilee is the familiar turf where the disciples got up early, fished all day, came home for dinner, played with the children, and fell asleep exhausted. Galilee is where they served with Jesus.

Easter's sequels are written in the ordinary places where we work, play, eat, and sleep. Jesus' story continues in everyday events—when we listen to a friend, take a walk, tell a joke, and discover the sacred in the midst of the routine. We are the disciples who have been sent to celebrate.

The Sunday school teacher asks, "When did Easter become important to you?"

An elderly woman answers slowly, "I didn't understand Easter until my husband died. When he died, I thought I died, too, but I was wrong. God still had some life for me. For twenty years God has been bringing life out of a dead person."

The table is set for a meal that never ends. Easter is unfinished business, expectations yet unfulfilled. Whenever life triumphs over death, whenever we feed the hungry, and whenever we live with grace, Easter continues. Whenever we care for the lonely, whenever we love another, and whenever we live with hope, the story goes on.

If God Is Here

Luke 24:13-35

When Jesus was at the table with them, he took bread,
blessed and broke it, and gave it to them. Then their eyes
were opened, and they recognized him; and he vanished
from their sight. (Luke 24:30-31)

You walk into worship and sit down beside a friend. Your pal, who should feel guilty for sleeping late on Sunday but does not, asks, "How was Sunday school?"

You start to tell how your teacher inspired you to give thanks for God's grace, but then you think of something else: "We had a visitor. She had the most curious shoes. They looked Dutch, like those wooden shoes women in Holland wear."

Your friend smiles, so you keep going. "She had blond hair cut in a Mary Tyler Moore 1970s flip. If she had been wearing suspenders and a blue plaid skirt, she could have been the woman on the Swiss Miss Hot Cocoa box."

Your friend giggles as you add, "And coincidentally, she had a little chocolate moustache." You try not to laugh out loud.

You have to stop being hilarious as the passing of the peace begins.

"The Lord be with you."

"And also with you."

The woman seated directly in front of you turns to greet you, and you are mortified. She has blond hair, but it doesn't look much like Mary's. She doesn't have a moustache, and though you can't see them, her shoes are probably normal.

The woman is smiling—sort of. You can't tell if she heard what you said. What did she hear? How much did you embarrass yourself? What *did* you say? Was what you said offensive? Why didn't you notice that she was right there?

The two from Emmaus asked, "How much did we embarrass ourselves? What *did* we say? Did we say anything offensive? Why didn't we notice that he was right there?"

On Easter Sunday afternoon, these two dejected disciples are walking home down a dusty road, their chins on their chests, their eyes blank, and their faces empty, still too stunned to think clearly.

They wish they could go back to the life they had before they met Jesus, but they know it will not be the same. Maybe things will be simpler now. The disciples never could keep up with Jesus. It crosses their minds that it will be easier to love a memory than to follow Jesus.

They do not even hear his footsteps. Jesus joins them and doesn't seem surprised that they don't recognize him. He asks what they've been talking about. They can hardly believe he doesn't know: "Where have you been? How can you not know what's been going on?"

They explain to the uninformed stranger that a prophet has been executed. Jesus was gracious in all that he did. He spoke as no one had ever spoken. When they were with him, they not only *felt* better but also wanted to *be* better.

They tell the stranger that Jesus' death is the death of their hopes. Some women are spreading a story about an empty tomb and angels, but they know despair when they feel it.

Jesus wonders how they can be so dense. "You haven't been paying attention."

He teaches them what the Scriptures say about how the Messiah must suffer. He lays it all out for them, and they don't get it. Jesus himself leads the Bible study, and nothing happens.

When they arrive home, the two disciples invite him to stay for supper. Jesus volunteers to say grace. He breaks bread and passes it to them. Scholars suggest that Luke has given us the order of worship for the early church. The preacher interprets the Bible, and then he blesses the bread and shares it.

In the middle of Communion, they realize Jesus is there. The first thing they say after he's gone is, "Didn't you feel something inside? Why weren't we more awake? Why didn't we recognize him? Why weren't we paying attention? If we had known Jesus was here, we would have listened more carefully. We wouldn't have wasted time jabbering on and on. We would have acted differently."

Everything is different when we recognize that God has come. My mother had a curse she used on me when I was a teenager leaving the house on a Saturday night: "Remember that God is watching you."

When you're seventeen, you don't want to hear, "God is watching you."

That's true when you're seventy, too. God is with us not only when we're kind but also when we're not, when we're hopeful and when we give up, when we're paying attention and when we're completely oblivious to God's presence. God is comforting, loving, and empowering, and God is challenging, calling, and pushing.

The news on the road to Emmaus is not only that we get to live in God's presence; it's also that we *have* to live in God's presence. God is forever pulling us from blindness to sight, from deafness to hearing, from the routine to the extraordinary.

If God is here, then it is not enough to be students of Scripture, not enough to support the church, not enough to be nice to one another. If God is here, then we need to share our lives with God.

If we believe that God is with us, then we have no business with business as usual. We are foolish to go a day without praying and wrong to hold grudges against sisters and brothers.

God is with us in our waking and our sleeping, our going to work and our coming home, our friendships and our families, our joys and our sorrows.

When Martin Luther was suffering one of his bouts with depression, he found himself tracing on the table with his finger the words, "He lives. He lives!"

You spend the prelude looking at the back of the head of the blond woman who is not from Switzerland. You feel terrible, but you decide not to think about how embarrassed you are until after worship. You will introduce yourself to the woman and say something nice about Mary Tyler Moore. As you sing "Jesus Christ Is Risen Today," you feel like it would be good if God raised you from the dead today.

You settle in to listen to the sermon, but the story distracts you. A tired pair walking home does not even notice that Jesus is with them. They chatter and babble like people do without imagining that Christ is present. He tries to open the Bible to them, but they're so caught up in their own thoughts that they don't hear what Jesus is saying.

Why can't they see that Christ is walking beside them? Jesus takes bread, blesses it, breaks it, and gives it to them. At the table, we see that Christ is with us.

STARTING AGAIN

ACTS 10:34-45

*They put Jesus to death by hanging him on a tree; but
God raised Jesus on the third day and allowed Jesus to
appear, not to all the people but to us who were chosen
by God as witnesses, and who ate and drank with Jesus
after the resurrection from the dead. (Acts 10:39-41)*

Easter is not for those who are satisfied with the way things are.
Many are content with the bad habits to which they have grown
accustomed. They don't see any reason to stop doing things just
because they aren't worth doing. But there are some things I need
to quit. I need to quit skipping breakfast; quit eating drive-thru food;
quit listening to talk radio (except NPR); quit checking e-mail twenty
times a day; quit copying pages I'm not going to read;
quit overestimating the importance of people who complain; quit
underestimating the importance of people who don't complain;
quit wishing I was taller, younger, or richer.

You've gotten used to some things that you shouldn't have gotten
used to. Quit nagging. Quit smoking. Quit eating too much. Quit
watching television shows that dull your mind. Quit reading
magazines that don't make you smarter. Quit playing poker on the
computer. Quit cheating on your taxes. Quit being so hard on others.
Quit being so hard on yourself. Quit dividing people into winners
and losers. Quit counting your money. Quit believing you deserve
everything you have. Quit wanting more. Quit feeling trapped in
what you've always done. Quit complaining about anything you're
not willing to work to fix. Quit thinking the problems of the world

aren't your responsibility. Quit accepting mediocrity. Quit waiting. Quit being afraid of anything that's new.

The good news of Easter is that we aren't stuck in the old ways. The promise of the resurrection is that we can change. Easter is for people who want something new.

Simon Peter wanted things to change. If he hadn't been dissatisfied with the way things were, we would never have heard of him. Simon was a fisherman who lived with his wife in Capernaum. They shared a house with his mother-in-law and his brother Andrew. Fishing wasn't the worst occupation, but there were mornings when Simon wished his boat had sunk during the night. The nets were always tangled. Simon smelled like tuna and his brother smelled like sardines. He was sick of sushi, and there are only so many ways to filet a fish. Simon had nightmares about tilapia.

Simon first laid eyes on Jesus on one of those days. Jesus said, "So you're Simon. I'm going to call you Peter the Rock."

Jesus was the change Peter had been waiting for.

"You should follow me," Jesus said. "Quit fishing. From here on out, people should be your business."

Peter dropped his nets and got on a first-century roller coaster. For three years Peter followed Jesus up and down and around curves he had never imagined. There were high points like the time Jesus responded to something Peter said with the only beatitude he ever made up for a single person: "Blessed are you, Simon. Flesh and blood has not revealed this to you, but my Father in heaven. Upon this rock I will build my church." There were low points like five minutes later, when Jesus told Peter, "Get behind me, Satan. You're a stumbling block."

Peter said the wrong things, asked the wrong questions, and got the wrong ideas, but he loved the ride. There was the time when Jesus was walking on the water. Peter got out of the boat and tried it for himself, but rocks don't float. Jesus had to play lifeguard and fish him out.

Peter was never sure where they were headed, but every day was exciting. Jesus preached, consoled, and infuriated. Peter blundered, misconstrued, and misunderstood, but he loved the life that Jesus brought.

Peter never looked back, until the end. On the night before the cross, he promised that he would lay down his life for Jesus, but after Jesus was arrested, Peter claimed three times that he did not even know him.

The world came to an end. At little more than thirty, Jesus was destroyed, made horribly dead. Tears ran down Peter's face like rain running off a rock.

On Easter Sunday morning, Jesus gave Peter a new start. Jesus told Peter to feed his sheep, and Peter did it. On Pentecost, the wind of the Spirit blew, and Peter preached, "God declares, I will pour out my Spirit upon all flesh, and your sons and your daughters will prophesy, and your young men shall see visions, and your old men shall dream dreams."

Given a new start, Peter stood up to the same power brokers that condemned Jesus. He said, "We cannot keep from speaking about what we have seen and heard."

The Jewish fisherman visited in the home of a Roman centurion, an officer of the occupying army. Cornelius wanted to join the church. The old law-abiding Peter would have sent the question to a committee, but he had caught the absolute joy of what the church is supposed to be. He almost exploded with the good news: "The gospel is for everybody. God plays no favorites. It makes no difference who you are or where you're from. If you want God to give you a new start, it's yours. The Spirit is drawing the poor, hungry, and oppressed. You know what happened in Judea. Jesus went through the countryside telling everyone that God offers a new way of life. The religious authorities liked the old way, so they hung him on a cross, but in three days, God had him up, alive, and telling those who would listen God's good news. Jesus broke bread and drank the wine of new life. Before long, hundreds of his followers had seen him. Our lives opened up like that tomb and flowed with fresh new passion. Folks who had been shut up in fear broke free into fierce new courage. People closed up in guilt emerged, not ashamed anymore. People sealed up in sadness stepped into the light laughing, singing, and embracing one another.

God raised Jesus from the dead to bring new life to you, to me, to the church, to all of us. We can start anew."

By the grace of God, we can begin again. I need to start trying new things; start seeing new visions; start dreaming new dreams; start letting go of old ideas; start eating salads; start kissing my wife good-bye every morning; start rolling down the window; start listening to the birds; start noticing the trees; start reading a poem a day; start reading the Bible as much as I read books about the Bible; start believing in starting again.

You need to start looking for good things to start. Start breathing deeply. Start appreciating little things you have never noticed. Start turning off your phone. Start exercising. Start keeping a journal. Start asking questions. Start drinking decaf. Start listening to someone else's music. Start calling your mother-in-law. Start telling more people more often that you love them. Start learning the names of your friends' children. Start looking poor people in the eye. Start giving others the freedom to start again. Start listening to the Spirit. Start imagining. Start laughing. Start celebrating. Start changing.

The good news of the joyous supper is that we can begin again. By the grace of God, we can start anew.

Giving So It Doesn't Hurt

ACTS 4:32–5:11

Then Peter said to Sapphira, "How is it that you have agreed together to put the Spirit of the Lord to the test? Look, the feet of those who have buried your husband are at the door, and they will carry you out." Immediately she fell down at his feet and died. (Acts 5:9-10)

Churches should read the story of Ananias and Sapphira before taking the offering. How would it affect church budgets if preachers told this story every Sunday?

The only picture I remember of this story was in a children's Bible. An extremely overweight Ananias is being carried out while Sapphira clutches her chest and falls backwards. There ought to be a warning on the book: "This contains a scene of graphic violence."

What would you think of reading this passage as a litany? The men could read Ananias's part and the women Sapphira's. One drawback is that Ananias has no lines and Sapphira has only, "Yes, that was the price," which doesn't sound like it would read well in unison. Luke, who wrote this story, knows how strange it is to have this hand grenade explode in the middle of Mother Goose.

Everything is fine and dandy in the early church. Pentecost has increased attendance. People in the church are learning how to watch out for one another.

A good man named Barnabas sells some property and gives the money to the benevolence fund. Sapphira and Ananias see the applause Barnabas receives and decide to sell some of their land and make a not-at-all-anonymous donation.

This couple's names are curious. Sapphira means "beautiful." Ananias can be translated "the Lord is gracious." Readers are supposed to catch the irony.

Ananias takes the check by the church office. Peter thanks Ananias for his gift by saying, "Ananias, why are you filled with the devil? What came over you to do such a thing? You're not just lying to us. You're lying to God."

Ananias drops dead. This scares the living daylights out of everyone. They lay a sheet over him, carry him outside, and bury him.

About three hours later, Sapphira starts wondering if Ananias has sneaked off to the golf course. She drops by the church without knowing what has happened.

Peter asks, "How much did you get for that land you sold?"

Peter does not sound like he is offering Sapphira a last chance to confess. The prosecuting attorney is making sure the perjury charge sticks. She nervously answers, "That's the right price," and Peter pronounces her dead: "We're about to bury you in the backyard, too."

In what has to be a gross understatement, Luke writes that fear seizes the whole church. Oddly enough, it is the first use of the word "church" in the book of Acts.

This harsh, severe, uncompromising, amazingly dispassionate story raises all kinds of questions.

When people make a donation to a church, they seldom hear, "Why has Satan filled your heart?"

This story is cruel. How do you bury a husband without telling his wife? Does a first offense call for death with no opportunity for an appeal? If Peter thinks there is a problem, shouldn't he talk to the couple in private? If Jesus didn't kill Judas at the Last Supper, how is this fair?

If they had been given a chance to defend themselves, Ananias and Sapphira would have said that they were only putting a little away for their children's education or their retirement. Maybe they were simply replacing what they lost in the last economic downturn. It doesn't seem worth the trouble to make a big deal out of the small percentage they kept. This story doesn't have a drop of mercy.

Scholars have gone to great lengths to explain it away. One guess has been that Ananias and Sapphira were the first Christians to die and that this story was the explanation to their fellow Christians about why they died and missed the expected return of Christ.

In recent years, psychological explanations have become popular. Perhaps the shock of exposure killed them. Maybe they had heart attacks because they felt so guilty. Maybe they dropped dead because they were afraid of Simon Peter. The whole story may be one crazy, bizarre, incredible coincidence.

The closest we can come to understanding this unexplainable story may be that the deaths of Ananias and Sapphira—as horrible as they are—are preferable to the death of Jesus' church. The couple's sin is not keeping part of the money. Their sin is pretending that their commitment to the church is purer than it is. The couple wants to appear to embody ideals that they have not accepted. Their concern for their reputation leads them to lie. Their attempt to look genuine threatens to infect the church with hypocrisy. If the spirit of pretense had become the spirit of the church, it would have been the death of the church. Dishonesty is deadly.

Masquerading as anything other than what we are destroys us from the inside. The life spent asking, "Do people think I'm important?" is wasted. Hypocrites die a slow death.

Passing ourselves off as anything that we are not is self-destructive. Jesus' strongest condemnation is of the Pharisees. He calls them hypocrites and actors. Insincerity is the deadliest sin.

The danger comes when we confuse reality and appearance. We begin to believe that what we want to look like is more important than what we actually are. We try to look concerned and compassionate rather than being concerned and compassionate. Everything is a performance—even when we are alone, even when the performance is just for ourselves. We act like people of faith instead of living our faith.

For the story of Ananias and Sapphira to make any sense, it has to include Barnabas. The early church prays for God to help them live with generosity. Barnabas is one of the answers to that prayer. He sells his land to help needy people. He has no ulterior motives and no desire for recognition. Barnabas proves that bona fide, authentic Christianity is a possibility. The church can really be the church.

Do we share our lives with authenticity? Do we genuinely worship, genuinely pray, genuinely listen, genuinely give, and genuinely care? Do we ask what God would have us do?

God asks us to live deeply and honestly from the depths of our hearts. We do not need to impersonate Christians. We can come to Christ's table as Christ's church. We can receive the bread and cup honestly. We can be Christians.

ATTENDING
YOUR OWN FUNERAL

ACTS 9:36-43

Peter knelt down and prayed. He turned to the body and said, "Tabitha, get up." Then she opened her eyes, and seeing Peter, she sat up. (Acts 9:40)

Before Darren and Samantha had their bewitched little girl, this most well-known Tabitha was a gracious woman whose full-time job was being a mother to everyone she knew and to some she did not know. She was the kind of woman every mother wants her son to marry and every old man wishes he had.

When Dorcas—the Greek version of Tabitha—becomes ill, her friends assume that this Proverbs 31 woman will be fine. How can anything bad happen to someone so good? How can *she* die when there are so many good-for-nothing people using up air?

When Dorcas passes away, they are heartbroken. They weep as they tenderly care for her body and lay her in her bed. Someone suggests that they send for Peter, who is eleven miles away.

The two volunteers are a mile down the road before they realize why they are going. They are getting the preacher for the funeral.

When Peter gets there, he goes upstairs and sees the women crying.

They are showing off clothing that Dorcas made for them: "She gave me this blouse for my birthday. Isn't the embroidery lovely?"

"And her needlepoint was so detailed."

"I remember one Sunday Dorcas noticed a tear in my sleeve. She got out a needle and thread and fixed it right there."

Peter doesn't know exactly what he's going to do, but he remembers Jesus and Jairus's daughter. Peter was confused and amazed by what happened then. Why can't he be confused and amazed again? What did Jesus do at Jairus's house? He cleared the room. Peter sends everyone downstairs and kneels to pray.

Luke, the one who wrote the story, was not there. When someone told him, Luke thought about toning it down and making it more believable, but he finally decided to tell the story the way he heard it and let people make up their own minds. Peter kneels and says, "Tabitha, get up."

Peter says it softly, because he does not want anyone to hear if she *does not* get up.

Dorcas attends her own funeral. She hears sobbing from the kitchen. She sees mascara running and the table covered with clothes that she made. She is so pleased to see her friends and family. She has not seen some of them in years. They hug and cry at the best funeral they have ever attended.

When we imagine our own funerals, we picture them like Dorcas's. Friends and family will come from miles around. Hearts will break. Mascara will run. Everyone we have known will be there to join the weeping chorus. People will talk about how wonderful we were, and how they wish we could be there to see how much we were loved.

Best of all, the few people who didn't recognize how wonderful we were will see how terribly wrong they were about us, and they'll feel awful about it.

The headline in the newspaper will read, "Saint Passes on to Glory."

Most funerals are not that grand. Attendance at funerals is down. Most of the chairs are usually empty.

Yogi Berra said, "If you don't go to other people's funerals they won't go to yours."

A grandson calls. "I'm sorry," he says. "It's so far. I can't get off work." His mother is disappointed, but she does not say anything. The widow worries that there won't be enough pallbearers. The minister doesn't have quilts to display that the deceased made for the residents of nursing homes. The family has trouble thinking of touching incidents.

At some deaths, the reading of the will takes longer than the eulogy, and it draws more attention. Sometimes nobody cries.

Obituaries tend to include information that makes the lives of the deceased seem inconsequential: when they were born, when they died, and where they were when they died; their occupation, their relatives, and the arrangements for burial. Obituaries don't usually say anything about how the deceased lived, what mattered to them, or what difference they made. Most obituaries make the dead sound like they hardly lived. That is often accurate.

Death is frightening because life seems incomplete, but we shouldn't worry that we will die, because that is guaranteed. We should be afraid that we will fail to live.

We know people who have almost died and, after surviving the crisis, see their lives differently. Everything becomes doubly precious. Every day is more important. Many would never accomplish half of what they get done if they had not faced their own death. People who realize that their days are numbered are more likely to live their days to the fullest.

Trappist monks used to greet one another by saying, "Remember that you will die." They believed that remembering their mortality would remind them to give themselves to that which is immortal.

Attending her funeral must have been a pivotal event in Dorcas's life. Even more than before, Dorcas spent her days preparing for her death, living to the fullest, and knowing that her next funeral would be her last. We only get so many days. If we knew we were going to die soon, would that lead us to cherish the time we have left?

The closing lines of James Kavanaugh's "Most of the Warriors" are disturbing:

Most of the warriors I knew have settled down to gardening and
the morning *Times*
Most of the warriors I knew have unsaddled their stallions and built
a fence in their backyard

Most of the warriors I knew have died before their time and are
forgotten
Save in the memory of their sons
And the dreams they seldom share
Finally content to stare and wonder.
(James Kavanaugh, "Most of the Warriors," *Maybe If I Loved*, New
York: E.P. Dutton, 1982, 37)

The first time I read the poem, it depressed me so much that I decided
that *was not* going to happen to me. I took out a legal pad and made
a list of dreams. This was going to be my bucket list of things I hope
to do before I die: "I'd like to dance at my children's weddings, since
there was no dancing at my *Baptist* wedding. I'd like to go to a Bob
Dylan concert, even though I won't be able to understand the words.
I'd like to visit Wrigley Field in Chicago and pretend I'm a Cubs fan."

I thought my list was off to a good start, but then I looked again.
What a pitiful list. Everything was inconsequential.

I tried again. I made a second list of what I need to do before I
die. I wrote, "I would like to love my wife passionately, with a love
that brings her joy. I'd like to be a good father. I would like to make
my sons laugh. I'd like to be a good friend, for a few people to know
that if they have troubles I'll be there. I would like to help Christ's
church look more like Christ. I would like for the Spirit to teach me
to live each day to the fullest. I would like to live like a Christian."

We are going to die, and this is what we should do about it: Look
for joy every day. Be patient with ourselves and others. Take risks. Be
courageous. Say what we mean. Whine less over the routine ups and
downs. Spend more time on what is important and less time on what
is insignificant.

Be good to our parents. Love our friends, and, as much as we can,
our enemies. Speak to strangers. Share what we have with the poor.

Show grace to those who show no signs of knowing grace. Pray
fervently. Live every day passionately in the hope of God. In the bread
and cup, we receive God's invitation to live to the fullest. We keep
getting second chances.

Ordinary Time

GOD'S GOOD IDEA

ACTS 2:1-21

When the day of Pentecost had come, they were all together in one place. And suddenly from heaven there came a sound like the rush of a violent wind, and it filled the entire house where they were sitting. (Acts 2:1-2)

"I know what you're thinking, but in spite of the way they look and the sounds you've been hearing, the choir is not drunk. I can assure you that the choir isn't drunk, because it's only eleven o'clock in the morning." That's how Peter starts his sermon on Pentecost. Peter clearly didn't have time to prepare. On the birthday of the church, God is the only one planning the party.

At the end of chapter 1 of the book of Acts, the disciples are getting organized. They choose a new person to fill the vacancy Judas left on the board of disciples. They select Matthias, a forgettable choice, by throwing dice.

They are together for ancient Israel's Thanksgiving feast. As the smell of roast lamb fills the upper room, the disciples talk about administrative matters and how best to go about the business of incorporating as a 501(c)3 organization. As they say grace over the gravy and dressing, pandemonium breaks loose.

Nothing about their preparations has prepared them for what happens. Suddenly there is the sound of a great wind, rumbling like a tornado, the mysterious and unpredictable wind that hovered over the water at creation.

They see what they have heard. Something like fire is dancing over their heads. John the Baptist said that Jesus "will baptize with the Holy Spirit and fire," and it looks like it's happening now. The disciples' ideas about a businesslike organization are shattered forever. Everything is coming loose.

The tourists who fill Jerusalem hear the commotion and rush to find out what in heaven's name is going on. The meeting in the upper room spills out into the street. People who have never been to a church business meeting are in the middle of a doozy.

Many churches make it sound like the Spirit is a warm, fuzzy feeling. Luke goes to great lengths to say that the Spirit is not merely something we feel inside. The Spirit is wind, fire, and public debate. The Spirit pushes the disciples out of the quiet upper room and into the noisy streets.

Luke's roll call makes it clear that everyone is there—Parthians, Medes, Elamites, and residents of Mesopotamia. Even the Cretans are on the list. To be a Cretan was to be a first-century "dweeb." The church claimed all kinds of ragtag charter members.

God breathes upon that company of disciples and declares that the church will overcome the usual divisions. Pentecost is an assault on segregation, nationalism, racism, sexism, classism, and every way in which we separate ourselves from one another. Everybody is invited. Pentecost is God's assertion that people who are completely different from one another can understand one another.

Understanding exactly what happens with the wind, fire, and foreign languages is hard. The people who are there aren't sure what happened. Some of them jump to a peculiar conclusion, though with all the confusion, it's not surprising that they think they smell alcohol.

Peter stands to defend the disciples. Less than two months earlier, Peter allowed the fear of a servant girl in a courtyard make him say things he would regret for the rest of his life. The Spirit breathes courage into the new person that Peter has become, and he preaches a sensational sermon. Acts has twenty-eight sermons that account for almost a third of the book. Sometimes sermons can seem dull, but Peter's certainly isn't. It's a sermon like Martin Luther King, Jr.'s *I Have a Dream* speech. Peter preaches a sermon that changes history: "We're filled with the Spirit, but it's not like being drunk. God is pouring out the Spirit on all kinds of people."

Sons and daughters will preach—young people. In Jewish culture, young people were not allowed to lead, but God says that the young share God's grace. The old will have visions, too. God speaks through the residents of nursing homes. And daughters—women lead God's people. And slaves—the poorest of the poor receive a full portion of God's love. Those who are never asked to say a few words at the microphone speak for God. God's church is where old and young, male and female, rich and poor celebrate grace together. A few of the disciples swallow hard.

Peter says that God comes with fire and smoke that will hide the sun and moon. God comes terribly and wonderfully, with blessing and judgment. The source of the wind is no soft touch that doles out new life through cheery smiles. God breathes life into the church through a mighty rush of wind because nothing less will get it started. The surge of the Spirit pushes the church out of the business meeting and into the neighborhoods and workplaces. The breath of God brings new worlds into being. Churches are born. Dry bones come to life. Berlin walls fall. Business-as-usual worlds are destroyed.

At Pentecost, God blows away old ideas. The main character in this story is not Peter. Luke offers no description, no character development, and not a word about what Peter is thinking. Luke emphasizes the wind, fire, whistles, and sparks. Luke makes it clear that the church is God's idea.

This story also makes it clear that the church is not all God hoped it would be. We keep making the disciples' initial mistake of trying to tame the Spirit. If you ask how the church began, many imagine a group of white men in suits seated at tables arranged in a square. Peter stands behind a microphone, turns on an overhead projector, and says, "Here are the keys to an effective organization: (1) competent programs, (2) solid financial resources, and (3) adequate facilities and parking."

Our plans for the church sound like plans for a business. We have committees, by-laws, and procedures. We ask questions that sound suspiciously like, "How do we get more people to come to our church instead of going to other churches?" We are less likely to honestly ask, "Which way is the Spirit leading?" When we are capable of intelligent planning and choose to work with elaborate organizational structures, we are in danger of thinking that the church is our idea.

If we learn to watch for such things, we will see signs that the wind is still blowing. When we see the church going beyond what we planned, we see the work of the Spirit.

The Spirit is present when we realize that God is watching to see what we do in worship; when we sing a hymn that takes us back or takes us forward; when we hear Scripture that was written for us; when we share the bread and cup and genuinely want to be the church. The Spirit is present when we look across the aisle and recognize that a casual acquaintance is a sister or brother; and when we realize that the people who are not in church, the ones who do not feel invited, are family, too. When we become more of whom we are meant to be, when we let God open our hearts, and when we realize that God is just getting started with us, the Spirit is at work.

The table is not the church's. The supper belongs to the Spirit of Christ. Communion goes beyond our plans. We share the bread and cup in the hope of living God's dreams.

BREAD FOR THE JOURNEY

1 KINGS 19:1-13

The angel of the Lord came a second time, touched Elijah, and said, "Get up and eat, otherwise the journey will be too much for you." (1 Kings 19:7)

In the contest between Elijah and the prophets of Baal to see whose God is the real deal, Elijah wins hands down. Ahab, the king of Israel, is not sure who to pull for. The prophet Elijah is Jon Stewart to his John Boehner. Ahab's foreign-born wife, Jezebel, is Ann Coulter to Elijah's late night gadfly. Ahab, the worst king Israel has ever had, keeps getting caught in the middle.

On Mount Carmel, the prophets of Baal pull out the stops to get their candidate to set fire to the sacrificial offering. Nothing happens. Elijah gives Yahweh the word and jumps back just in time. Lightning flashes and the homecoming bonfire is on. The onlookers are beside themselves with enthusiasm.

We might think the euphoria from such an event would last for days, but it ends quickly. Queen Jezebel vows to get even with Elijah for what he has done to her crowd. Jezebel goes on the offensive, and Elijah is afraid.

The ones who saw Elijah on Mount Carmel find it hard to believe. This unflinching, unflappable man who has fought for Yahweh and won is scared—this man who prophesied drought and watched enemies' crops wither; who prayed for rain and saw it come in a thunderstorm; who snatched the Phoenician widow's boy from death; who stood before the king and was not afraid; and who confronted the priests of Baal and put their sun god to shame. This man who passes out miracles like they are going out of style is frightened. Elijah runs for his life. He does not stop running until he collapses in utter exhaustion and cries, "I've had enough, God. Take my life."

We may never use those words, but we know about despair. Do you ever feel tired without having worked hard? Do you ever feel like you need a break when you are on a break?

A schoolteacher doesn't return her students' papers for two weeks. They sit in a pile on her desk, but she can't muster the energy to look at them. An insurance adjuster listlessly prepares to go to work. He sits in his car for fifteen minutes, unable to summon the will to turn the key. A teenager is at home on Friday night, staring at the television, not because she has nowhere else to go but because doing nothing seems easier. A church member sits through a worship service without singing or hearing much of anything. Jesus promises rest for the weary because we get weary.

What does God do in response to Elijah's despair? God does not give Elijah a vision. God gives him toast and a glass of water. "Elijah, have a bite to eat. You'll feel better."

Elijah's journey back to wholeness begins with a simple response to God's simple invitation: "Get up and eat because this journey is too great for you."

The invitation is extended at every Communion table. Jesus first offered this hope to discouraged disciples. He knew that they couldn't make it alone, so he gave them bread and the grace to be whole.

God tells Elijah to go to Horeb, the Mountain of God. Half healed and unaware of what God is up to, Elijah hides in a cave. But God does not leave him alone. Up to this moment, Elijah has been too depressed to hear God. In the gentle stillness, though, he hears God ask, "How are you doing, Elijah?"

Elijah feels like he is the only good one left: "God, it's only you and me now."

Who hasn't felt like that? Haven't you felt like you are the only person with any sense? Do you ever think you are the only one in your family who cares? Are you the only one in the church who knows what the church should be doing? Do you long for the day when someone else sees things your way? Does life feel hopeless?

God reminds Elijah who is in charge. A tremendous storm sends rocks tumbling down the mountain. The wind almost blows Elijah off his feet. An earthquake nearly knocks Elijah silly. Another fire breaks out. Those are the ways Elijah expects God to speak, but he hears not a peep out of Yahweh. God is in the silence. Only when the fireworks are finished and a terrible hush falls over the mountain does Elijah hear something. What he hears is so much like silence that only through the ear of faith does he know that it is God. In the Hebrew, God speaks in "a voice of gentle stillness." God listens to Elijah's complaints and worries. Elijah hears now because, for the first time, he is still enough to listen to the still, small voice of Grace.

When we are still, God heals our frustration, clears our cloudy visions, and helps us see things as they are. Despair happens when we take ourselves too seriously and fail to take God seriously enough. Remembering that God is with us is recognizing that we still have hope.

An orderly works in a nursing home caring for the aged and incurably ill. To the average person it would be a drab job, but this orderly performs his tasks with surprising dignity. He takes genuine pride in his work. He handles the crotchety old men with gentleness. When patients have to be moved to the hospital for surgery, this orderly travels with them in the ambulance, even during his off-duty hours. If one is dying, the orderly stays at the bedside. This young man is a friend to people who have no one to love them. Their eyes light up when he comes into the room. He makes their last days of loneliness more tolerable. His life is an act of grace because he listens for God and remembers that he is never alone.

When we are still, we hear God ask, "Why do you have such an attitude? Why do you resent that person? What are you missing?"

God asks us the same question God asks Elijah: "How are you doing?"

The schoolteacher who can't look at the papers on her desk, the insurance adjuster who can't turn the ignition key, the teenager staring blankly at the television, and the church member who doesn't truly worship can learn to listen to the silence. God speaks to us, especially in our weariness. In the simple response of taking bread and cup, we accept God's gift of quiet hope. At the table, God offers strength for the journey.

GETTING IT ALL TOGETHER

LUKE 8:26-39

Jesus then asked him, "What's your name?" He said, "Legion"; for many demons had entered him. (Luke 8:30)

Jesus' boat lands on the eastern shore of the Sea of Galilee—no longer in Jewish territory. This is like landing in Cuba. Along the edge of the lake, tombs are cut into the mountain. The village graveyard is this land's version of a mental institution.

In Mark's Gospel, the story takes place at night. This place would have been spooky even in broad daylight. At night, it must have been terrifying. A howling man runs out of the tombs to greet them. He has been buried alive, banished to die in the cemetery.

The first-century world was different. Whatever we think about demons, they were intensely real to these people. Demons were responsible for every physical ailment. One Jewish rabbi estimated that there are seven and a half million demons. They believed that demons lived in unclean places like the graveyard, and drowning was the primary way to destroy them. Demons were especially dangerous to women in childbirth, children who were out after dark, and the newly married.

The ancient ideas may seem silly, but when the biblical writers speak of being possessed by demons, they use strikingly appropriate terms. Modern psychology has given the old demons new names like "paranoia" and "schizophrenia," but the old names correspond more closely to what people feel. Deeply conflicted people do not feel like they have a chemical imbalance. They feel possessed by a power that has taken control. When we are depressed, we do not feel like we have a vitamin deficiency; we feel overwhelmed.

Some mental illnesses can be effectively treated, and some cannot. With medication, many people can function well as physicians, accountants, and teachers. Others are possessed by what seems to be a legion of demons. Everyday life proves too much, and finally the family decides to send the afflicted person to a place where he or she can receive proper, constant care. The Gerasenes sent their mentally ill to the cemetery.

The man with good reasons to believe in demons runs at Jesus and shouts at the top of his lungs, "What have you got against me, Holy Child? Please don't mess with me."

Jesus feels compassion for this broken man who is half shackled and completely ostracized. When Jesus asks his name, the man answers, "Legion."

This person is so pulled apart that he feels like a mob of a thousand.

If a story this peculiar can have a most peculiar part, it is the detail about the pigs. As the man screams, a herd of pigs stampedes into the lake. Commentators suggest that the man's yelling frightens the swine, and they become the proof that he needs. He would never have believed that he was cured without visible evidence.

The herders in charge of the pigs run to tell others what has happened. They don't see a person healed; they see those pigs, that livelihood, stampeding to their deaths, costing someone a lot of money. "It wasn't our fault. Really, you've got to believe us. It wasn't our fault."

The people come to take a look and find the former mental patient sitting at the feet of Jesus. We might guess that the Gerasenes would invite Jesus to stay, but they ask him to leave at once.

Jesus, who was often willing to shake the dust off his feet, gets back into the boat without a word and prepares to set sail. The healed man looks at Jesus and then at the crowd who had banished him to the graveyard. "Please, let me go with you!" he pleads to the Lord.

There is room in the boat. This man will leave without looking back. There is no one who has not already told him good-bye.

But then he thinks about his family: "Will my wife take me back? Will my children call me 'Daddy' again? What will they say when they see I've been healed? Will they have trouble believing it?"

As these thoughts flash through his mind, Jesus says, "Go home. Tell them about God's love."

The man goes and tells how *Jesus* put his life back together.

Luke shares this story as a description of the grace that holds our lives together. God comes to us in our conflict and confusion and offers a sense of purpose. Our name does not have to be "Legion"; we can be "Christian."

An evil spirit destroys the hope of a single purpose by pulling us in a thousand directions. We want this and that and the other thing. We constantly have to choose between work and home, this commitment and that one, helping others and taking a break, what we want to do and what we need to do, what is good and what is better.

The psychologist Sam Keen wrote this in his journal:

There are so many lives I want to live, so many styles I would like to inhabit. In me sleeps Zorba the Greek's concern to allow no lonely woman to remain comfortless. (Here am I, Lord, send me.) Camus' passion to lessen the suffering of the innocent, Ernest Hemingway's drive to live and write with lucidity, and the unheroic desire to see each day end with tranquility and a shared cup of tea. I am so many, yet I may be only one. I mourn for all the selves I kill when I decide to be a single person. Decision is a cutting off. I travel one path only by neglecting many. So I turn my back on small villages I will never see, strange flesh I will never touch, ills I will never cure, and I choose to be in the world as a husband and a father. (*Twentieth Century Pulpit*, ed. James W. Cox [Nashville: Abingdon, 1981] 2:26)

We get frustrated when we can't travel all the roads at once. To quote the mystic Yogi Berra, "When we come to a fork in the road, we want to take it."

We don't want to focus on one thing. Making up our minds is hard.

Do you ever think you should have been a doctor or a cowboy or a talk show host? Do you have troubling ordering in restaurants? No matter what you order, do you catch yourself looking at what other people are eating and then wondering if you made a mistake? Does it take you thirty minutes to choose a flavor at Baskin-Robbins? Do you end up eating your butter brickle and wishing it were rocky road?

We are constantly forced to do this or that but not both. We feel like we should start jogging and read the best-sellers and meditate thirty minutes a day and learn French and cook healthier meals. We want to be good employees, good friends, good neighbors, and a good deal more rested than we are. We want to be Christians, and we want to be a lot of other things, too.

God offers the grace that holds our lives together. If we center our lives in God, then love becomes the criterion by which we choose. God makes grace the Maypole around which everything dances.

In his right mind, the healed man sits at the feet of Jesus. Letting God teach us to love is a step toward sanity. When life is good and we have a dozen options in front of us, we need God's grace to sort through the possibilities. When life is hard and we have a dozen difficulties to deal with, God's love makes sense of them.

When we eat the bread of hope, God offers love that gives direction. When we drink the cup of thanksgiving, we promise that the grace of God will hold us.

A PLACE AT THE TABLE

LUKE 10:38-42

But the Lord answered her, "Martha, Martha, you are worried and distracted by many things; there is need of only one thing. Mary has chosen the better part, which will not be taken away from her." (Luke 10:41-42)

Sometimes it's easier to be a man. Your last name is not an issue. Wedding plans take care of themselves. Mechanics tell you the truth. You never have to drive to another gas station restroom because this one is "just too icky." Three pairs of shoes are more than enough. The same hairstyle lasts for years. You get extra credit for the slightest act of thoughtfulness. Being a woman can be harder. It would be especially hard to be a woman in charge of a dinner party when Jesus is coming.

This dinner party is turning into a nightmare for Martha. She loves Jesus, but he never sticks to a schedule. He pops in all of a sudden, and Martha has to throw a meal together. Somehow she always pulls it off. This time Jesus is on his way to Jerusalem for mysterious big doings. Martha is on the spot again. She rushes, fusses, cooks, and cleans. She does so without anyone lifting a finger to help.

Not even Jesus lends a hand in setting the table or pouring the drinks; instead, he has all her other would-be helpers sitting spellbound at his feet, listening to him while the pot roast withers and the salad wilts. Lots of things are bothering Martha. What bothers her most is the way her little sister is acting like a man.

Mary is right in the middle. To sit at someone's feet is to be that rabbi's student. Women are not allowed to be students. As people wander through the kitchen, Martha hears them whisper, "Look where Mary is. What is that girl thinking? Mary knows she doesn't belong there."

Teaching a woman to read was illegal. Women were viewed as property. The rabbis taught that daughters were a curse and that the purpose of women was to bear sons. Only the man could initiate divorce. Women were excluded from the inner courts in the temple. Men did not speak to their wives in public, and yet Mary is at Jesus' feet, raising her hand and asking questions. Everyone is thinking the same thing: Mary ought to be in the kitchen.

Everyone except Jesus. Jesus knows the laws against rabbis teaching women, but he breaks those rules. Jesus speaks to a Samaritan woman at a well, and his disciples almost have a coronary. Jesus travels with women who support him financially. A friend of mine bravely titled a sermon, "Jesus was a Ladies' Man."

When Martha asks Jesus to tell Mary to get in her place, Jesus says that she has found her place: "Martha, you worry too much. Only one thing is necessary, one dish, a simple meal, and one place to give your attention."

If this is not our favorite Bible story, it may be because we are not Martha or Mary. We have no reason to believe that Jesus would say to us what he said to Martha. We do not spend much time in the kitchen. Someone is buying all those toaster pastries and frozen pizzas. We also don't think that Jesus would commend us as he did Mary. Few of us have learned to sit at Jesus' feet and be his disciples.

We need to hear this word because, like Martha, we may be guilty of discouraging others from taking a place at Jesus' feet. The rightful place of women is still an issue. In our society, women are more likely to be exploited or abused. Women are still underpaid, but we do not tend to get upset until it is our wife, daughter, or us. Listening to talk radio or rap music makes it clear that male chauvinism is still in style.

The church has been at the center of arguments for equal rights. For centuries, the church has distorted the gospel and denied the equality of women. The message of the Scriptures on how men and women are to relate to one another is extraordinarily complex, reflecting our experience. A few passages speak negatively toward women in leadership. In one place, Paul says that women in the Corinthian church should remain silent. He also says that women should not braid their hair, preach without their heads covered, wear jewelry, or cut their hair short. Some have drawn from these passages the sweeping conclusion that women should not serve in leadership roles, but we can't make the Bible say that.

For there are texts of Holy Scripture in which God calls women to ministry. The same Paul who tells women to keep silent assumes that women will preach. Philip's daughters preach in Caesarea. The word for deacon is used of the woman Phoebe. Women preach and pray in public, head house churches, serve as Paul's coworkers, and are persecuted and jailed just like men.

In the society of Paul's day, it was taken for granted that the male was superior to the female, the Jew to the Greek, and the free person to the slave. Paul catches a vision of a kingdom without prejudice— "no Greek nor Jew, no slave nor free, no male nor female in Christ Jesus."

If we draw our conclusions from the complete witness of Scripture, we understand that God calls women to any ministry God chooses.

We don't always recognize that the equality of women and men is not a peripheral issue. This concern is about how the Spirit speaks to half the world. If any of us are denied full partnership in the work of the church, then we all miss God's grace. Any way in which women are treated as second-class people is contrary to the gospel. Those who follow Jesus cannot discriminate.

Like Martha, we get distracted with things other than listening to Jesus and do not see that Jesus calls all of us because we need each other. When we fail to hear the voices of all God's people, then we fail to hear all that God is saying. We easily miss the gospel's revolutionary word that we are equal in God's family.

Jesus says, "Only one thing is necessary. Take a seat at my feet and listen." Jesus invites us to take our place at a table at which we are equals. We come to the supper together, as sisters and brothers. Jesus offers the bread and cup to all God's children.

Asking, Seeking, Knocking

Luke 11:1-13

"So I say to you, ask, and it will be given to you; search, and you will find; knock, and the door will be opened for you." (Luke 11:9)

Some people deserve more admiration than they usually get—nurses, foster parents, school bus drivers, and people who go to church. Churchgoers have to get moving on Sunday morning. Most dress up. Many get children ready. Some drive pretty far. They go to this trouble and then, much of the time, the reward is hearing what they are doing wrong.

Preachers get tired of repeating what Jesus says we ought to be doing. We wish there were more Sundays when the text is Jesus saying, "You're fine the way you are. Don't change a thing. You're just perfect."

Instead, we come to church and are told to share the story of Jesus with our neighbors, but we have trouble remembering the neighbors' names. We hear that we should care for strangers, but it is hard enough to care for the people we live with. We come to church and God calls us to love the whole world, but the world is not always loveable.

Coming to church is demanding, and yet people keep showing up. How can you not admire that? Following Jesus is hard. Jesus is an overwhelming example. Nobody is going to mistake us for Jesus any time soon.

People who try to live for Christ have good reasons to be discouraged. The needs of the world are so big and our resources so limited. If we love the world the way God calls us to love the world, our hearts will end up broken, because the world does not seem to be getting better.

Following Christ has always been difficult. In Luke 11, the disciples have been wandering around the countryside for three years. They never know where their next meal is coming from. They are making powerful enemies. Jesus says that the kingdom is coming, but the disciples see problems coming.

As Jesus finishes praying, one of the disciples asks, "Would you teach us to pray?"

Jesus answers, "When you pray, say this: Father, let us hallow your name by the way we live as well as by the words we speak. Let your kingdom come. Set the world right. Keep us all alive with three square meals. Keep forgiving us, and we'll keep forgiving everyone else. Keep us safe from ourselves and all evil."

The disciples think, "He's not making this any easier. We've been praying for God to set the world right, and it isn't happening. Forgiving everyone is way too much to ask. Keeping our distance from all evil doesn't sound like much fun either."

Jesus tries again: "Think of prayer this way. Suppose a friend shows up unexpectedly at midnight. He's been on the road all day and half the night with nothing to eat, so what are you going to do? You're going to get up and put something on the table. But what if you don't have anything? The refrigerator is empty. The cupboard is bare.

"Next door is your typical first-century Palestinian friend bedded down in his typical first-century Palestinian one-room house. Mom, dad, six children, half a dozen chickens, the dog, and a goat are sleeping in the same room. If they had more money, they would build a spare bedroom for the goat. You knock on his door.

"The friend answers from his bed, 'Don't bother me. The door's locked. My children are down for the night. Go home.' But you keep pounding on the door. Even if he won't get up because he's a friend, he'll finally get up and give you bread because if you keep knocking, you'll wake up the dog and then everyone is finished sleeping for the night."

Jesus' point is that the Christian life is about perseverance. Keep at it. Keep praying what you believe are God's hopes, and even if nothing comes, keep praying again and again.

Jesus wants to make it clear. "Here's what I'm saying. Ask and you'll get. Seek and you'll find. Knock and the door will open. Ask God for what the world needs. If your little boy asks for fish, do you scare him with a snake? If your little girl asks for an egg, do you trick her with a spider? As bad as you are, you wouldn't think of such a thing."

These words can be discouraging, too. If we pray believing that we will receive what we ask for, then it may be hard to keep praying when we do not. Sometimes when our prayers do not get answered, it is easier not to pray.

But Jesus says, "Don't you think that God who loves you will give the Spirit when you ask?"

We keep at it because Jesus promises that God will be with us. We work for what is right because those who are buried with Christ in baptism will be raised by the power of God. We pray and do not give up because God will take care of it all in the end.

We pray because changing the world is not our business; it's God's. Our business is to live with charity, do works of compassion, and know that the ultimate outcome is in God's hands. Our business is to do what we can, where we can, when we can, and to witness that God's kingdom is coming bit by bit, step by step, even in us.

When we pray, it is not to inform God what needs to be done. Prayer is taking our place with God no matter what comes. We pray because we've been promised that at the end of all the struggles, God will fill our deepest hunger.

Sarah Miles is a former atheist who is the director of the food pantry at St. Gregory's Episcopal Church in San Francisco. She calls it the "Church of the One True Sack of Groceries." As a journalist, she covered the 1980s wars in Central America up close where people were dying, and later she became an editor for the investigative magazine *Mother Jones*. After that, she found herself walking into St. Gregory's Church.

Here is how she describes her conversion:

> I was just curious. I'm a reporter. I'm curious. I like to poke my
> nose in places, and I walked into this building thinking, "Huh,
> wonder what's going on in there?" I had wandered into a church
> that offers communion to everyone, including strangers. A woman
> put a piece of fresh bread in my hand and gave me a goblet of some
> rather nasty, sweet wine. I ate the bread and was completely
> thunderstruck by what I felt happening to me. So I stood there
> crying, completely unsure of what was happening. I got out of the
> church as quickly as I could before some strange, creepy Christian
> would try to chat with me, and came back the next week because I
> was hungry, and kept coming back and kept coming back to take
> that bread. I think what I discovered in that moment when I put
> the bread in my mouth and was so blown away by the reality of
> Jesus was that the requirement for faith turned out not to be
> believing in a doctrine, or knowing how to behave in a church, or
> being the right kind of person, or being raised correctly, or repeating
> the rituals. The requirement for faith seemed to be hunger. It was
> the hunger that I had always had and the willingness to be fed by
> something I didn't understand. (Religion and Ethics Newsweekly,
> PBS, May 25, 2007)

If we go to God hungry for anything less than God, we may come
away empty. If we go to God hungry for God, we will come away
with the deepest of our hungers filled. So we keep coming to the table
to be fed by God, because at the heart of all our prayers, God is what
we are praying for.

One Lord, One Faith, One Baptism

Ephesians 4:1-6

*One Lord, one faith, one baptism, one God and Father
of all, who is above all and through all and in all.
(Ephesians 4:5-6)*

A Baptist writing on Christian unity is like Lance Armstrong writing on ethics. For most of our four hundred years, Baptist contributions to Christian unity would fit in a thimble and still rattle around like a BB in a boxcar. Baptists are terrible at getting along with each other, much less getting along with other Christians who aren't Baptists.

Baptists are not good at Christian unity, but you can make a case that most believers are not. In the Scriptures, we find such wonderful words: "One Lord, one faith, one baptism, one God above all and through all and in all." But when we close the Bible and look at the church, it is not happening. Paul's high-sounding words in Ephesians, "one body and one Spirit," do not describe our present situation. Far from being one body, the church has divided and subdivided many times.

Let your fingers stroll through the church section of the *Yellow Pages*. Most big cities have African Methodist Episcopal, Anglican, Apostolic, Assemblies of God, Baptist, Catholic, Charismatic, Christian (Disciples of Christ), Christian Methodist Episcopal, Christian Missionary Alliance, Christian Science, Church of Christ, Church of God, Church of God in Christ, Church of God Seventh Day, Church of Jesus Christ of Latter-day Saints, Church of the Living God, Church

of the Nazarene, Episcopal, Evangelical—still only up to the E's—
Foursquare Gospel, Friends, Full Gospel (not a compliment to the rest
of us), Greek Orthodox, Independent, Interdenominational, Jehovah's
Witnesses, Lutheran, Mennonite, Methodist (churches with "United"
or "Free" in their name are seldom united or free), Metropolitan
Community, Non-denominational, Pentecostal, Presbyterian, Russian
Orthodox, Seventh-day Adventist, Unitarian, and United Church of
Christ (as if there is such a thing).

John Calvin thundered, "There cannot be two or three churches
unless Christ is torn asunder," and then Calvin started his own
denomination. The "one body" has been dismembered with arms and
legs strewn all around.

The church is divided, but it doesn't bother us much. If we think
about Christian unity at all, it is as the punch line to a joke. During
an ecumenical gathering, a secretary rushes in, shouting, "The
building is on fire!" The Baptists yell, "Where is the water?" The
Methodists gather in the corner to pray. The Quakers quietly thank
God for the blessing of fire. The Roman Catholics pass the plate to
cover the damage. The Episcopalians form a processional and march
out. The Christian Scientists conclude that there is no fire. The
Presbyterians appoint a chairperson who is to appoint a committee
to look into the matter and bring a written report. The secretary grabs
the fire extinguisher and puts the fire out.

We hope that God smiles over our differences, because the dark
side of our divisions is that we have learned to measure other groups
by how close they are to our group. We assume that God does the same
thing.

We find it easy to define orthodoxy as our doxy and heresy as
everyone else's ideas. We get used to our hymns, traditions, and
provincialism. When some of us were growing up, we were taught to
be friendly, but in religious matters we were told to keep our distance
from other flavors of Christians. We acted as if they had something that
might be catching. When my mother said "mixed dating," it meant
going to a movie with a Methodist. We thought of ourselves as a team
competing against the other teams. Maybe we bought into the
American idea that competition is good for everyone—"free-enterprise

religion." Slowly but surely, we came to think that the boundaries we created had always been there. The walls we build seem permanent.

But we shouldn't be confident about the lines we've drawn. Paul Tillich said that to "speak of the divine properly, you have to stutter." Is it really our job to mark the boundaries?

Father Joseph and I were talking about which of our two churches was more welcoming to other Christians.

I said, "Joe, if I came to your church, you wouldn't let me share Communion." If we were playing chess, I would have added, "Check."

But then Father Joe countered, "If after a lifetime as a Christian minister, I went to a Baptist church, most of them would insist that I be baptized again."

"Checkmate."

A woman grows up in a Baptist church, serves as a faithful member, and decides to marry an Orthodox Jew. She plans to convert to Judaism. The members of the Baptist church have to think about how they feel about her decision. The pastor decides to have a public discussion of what her choice might mean. The people in the church talk about the meaning of faith, the importance of doctrine, and the breadth of God's love.

Finally, someone says, "There's just a lot we don't know. We need to leave what we don't know to God. There are things I believe with all my heart. I'm committed to what I think are important truths. But the boundaries, whatever boundaries there are, belong to God."

The lines are not as clear as we would like them to be, and the lines get in the way. Mother Teresa said, "If you judge people, you have no time to love them."

What is at the heart of what we believe? In our best moments, the center of our hope is the one true God who draws us together. The division in the church does not trouble us, but it bothers St. Paul. He writes, "We were all baptized by one Spirit into one body—and we were all given the one Spirit to drink . . . because there is one loaf, we who are many, are one body, for we all partake of one loaf."

Paul argues that if there is one God, then there must be one body— one church into which everyone is invited, one spirit that brings life, one hope that unites us, one baptism that invites us to oneness, and one God above all and through all and in all.

Jesus said that whoever is not against us is for us. The boundaries we draw are more narrow and concrete. Jesus talked about sheep that are not of this flock. As God's people, we should accept those who hold views other than our own in a spirit of Christian tolerance. We don't need the kind of tolerance that accepts anything because we don't care what is right. Instead, we need the spirit that understands that, as human beings, we don't know everything, and people who hold different views should be accepted in the spirit of Christ.

I spent a couple of wonderful days at a Catholic retreat center. When I checked in, I told one of the ministers that I would like to come to Mass and that I understood that I should not take Communion.

She said, "No, please share Communion with us."

I was surprised. "Thank you, I didn't realize that was okay."

She smiled. "Well, after all, no one will know who you are."

The truly good news of grace is that no matter who we are, God welcomes us to the table. God delivers us from meager hearts so that we will not exclude anyone whom God welcomes.

THE CONTINUING
CONVERSATION OF FAITH

JOHN 6:35, 41-51

"I am the living bread that came down from heaven.
Whoever eats of this bread will live forever; and the
bread that I will give for the life of the world is my flesh."
(John 6:51)

When St. Augustine was asked a question about astrology, he responded that his main quarrel with the practice is not that it is superstitious, which it is (of course I would think that; I am a Pisces). Augustine said that astrology is a lie because it claims to have simple answers for complicated questions. The great saint had such respect for the complexity of life that he had contempt for easy solutions. Most people love simple answers: the three causes of World War II; the four reasons nachos should be considered health food; the five ways Batman is not as good as he used to be. We are forever pinning things down, explaining things, and fixing things in our minds. We should not make faith appear simpler than it is. Our job is not to explain God, Jesus, or Christianity. Our calling is to be part of a continuing conversation with God.

The stories of Jesus cannot be summarized in succinct statements. Jesus is in a huge crowd when someone asks him, "How do we get food for all of these people? Two hundred silver pieces wouldn't be enough to buy each one half a sandwich."

A little boy's lunch is presented to illustrate the meagerness of their resources—five small barley loaves and two fish. Jesus gives thanks, and five thousand eat their fill.

"Gather up the leftovers," Jesus says, "so that even those who show up late can have a plate."

This peculiar story should not be explained away too simply. Whatever happened, the crowd is amazed. They follow him around the Sea of Galilee, but not because they are anxious to hear what he has to say.

They want another free meal: "Do what you did before. This time, could you grill the fish in a lemon sauce? Sourdough bread would be nice."

Jesus tells them not to work for food that spoils but to pay attention to food that lasts forever. The connection between the bread they have eaten and eternity is unclear, so they ask him to explain. Jesus says, "I am the bread of life. Whoever eats this bread will never die."

For two thousand years, Jesus' followers have tried to make everything Jesus said seem more reasonable than it often sounds. "Eat my flesh and you will never die" is a strange thing to say. Who wouldn't be confused?

What would be our reaction? A street preacher shouts, "Step right up. Get your bread from heaven. Anyone who eats this will never die."

This is beyond Jimmy Swaggart sweating, Benny Hinn crying, and Joel Osteen grinning. Jesus sounds like a snake oil salesman. The theological sophisticates of the Hebrew Divinity School of Jerusalem complain, "What kind of nonsense is this? What would your parents think if they heard this foolishness?"

Jesus does not respond to that, but he says something about being drawn to God. Again he brings up the bread from heaven that leads to life. The conversation is hard to follow. Jesus uses phrases that need to be explained but doesn't explain them.

What bothers the listeners most is not the difficulty of understanding Jesus. It's Jesus' claim that *they* need *his* help. Jesus is most offensive to those who think they can figure faith out on their own. "Isn't this the carpenter whose family we've known for years? We're better educated than Jesus."

If faith is about knowledge, then Jesus is unnecessary, because there is more than enough religion to argue about. Faith is still mistakenly defined as a set of beliefs. Jesus teaches that faith is an ongoing search for meaning, our response to the way God pulls us toward God's self. Faith is not an accomplishment but a gift. Belief is not an achievement but grace. God subtly pulls us along, offering flashes of illumination as we travel the dark path, placing within us the feeling that we are not alone and not yet home.

We think we know where we are going, but are we sure? How lost are we? Where are we being drawn?

Faith is not unwavering knowledge. Faith is being in conversation with God, being drawn to a God we do not fully understand. Faith is more like a novel than a textbook. You can read a math book, think about it, and work at it until you get it: "The square root of 225 is 15." When you read a great novel, you come out with your life changed and your way of viewing the world transformed. At the end of a great novel, you do not say, "I got it." Instead, it has gotten you.

We need God, but we want to act like we don't. We want to pray, but we don't want to be hypocrites. We want to be independent, but we don't want to be alone. We want to belong, but we want to be ourselves. We believe, and we are filled with unbelief.

God offers the bread of life because we don't completely understand: "This is the bread that has come down from heaven so that we can be taught by God."

The bread of life is an ongoing dialogue with God that becomes the best part of who we are. Eating this bread is accepting this conversation into our hearts. The bread of life is the willingness to be in dialogue with the often difficult story of Christ. Our ability to explain is not the point. The point is to be in the conversation, listen carefully, and be drawn to the table by the grace of God. After everything has been said about the Lord's Supper, just as with faith itself, still more remains.

HEALING

Out of the depths I cry to you, O LORD.
LORD, hear my voice! (PSALM 130:1-2)

Laura is a married mother of two, a boy and a girl. One morning in the shower, she feels a lump in her breast. She wants to ignore it, but she knows that's not much of a long-term strategy. A few days later, she hears her doctor say, "We need to run some tests."

For the longest time, she doesn't tell anyone except her husband about the cancer, but when she begins treatment, she tells the people at her church.

They say, "We'll be praying for you." A few encourage her to pray as if she *knows* that God will heal her. The subtle implication is that she has to believe that she will be healed, or it will not work. Faith sounds like denial.

They keep telling Laura, "You're looking good," which is a nice compliment, but the question "Compared to what?" pops into her head.

An older woman says that back in her mother's day, this kind of cancer was a death knell. They have made so many advances, and isn't Laura lucky that she doesn't have to do the really bad kind of chemo.

Is there a good kind of chemo?

The hushed tone in which they ask, "How are you?" becomes unnerving. She wishes she could say, "The treatment is making me constipated, but thanks for asking." Instead she replies, "Okay, I guess."

People keep telling her how brave she is. What choice does she have?

She gets a lot of, "You can beat this. You can win. You're tough."

She feels guilty about it, but she starts to resent a few people. They mean well, but they must not be able to hear what they're saying.

What are they thinking when they imply that this is an educational exercise?

"God means this for good, Laura."

How dare a healthy person suggest that cancer is in her best interest? As a self-improvement strategy, suffering is overrated.

Laura fleetingly considers slapping the woman who says, "You know God doesn't put more on us than we can carry."

Taken to its logical conclusion, this theory suggests that Laura and her children would be better off if Laura were a weaker person.

What about this one? Someone actually quotes, "The Lord giveth and the Lord taketh away." Who wants to worship a God who takes a mother, wife, and daughter away from the people who need her?

And, worst of all, another says, "We know this is God's will," which makes God sound horrible, choosing to give Laura cancer and remove hair and body parts she would rather have kept.

A man she doesn't know well sends out an e-mail that begins, "Dear Prayer Warriors, I know that you believe that God heals, so I'm writing to ask you to pray for our friend Laura."

She can't explain why it makes her uneasy, but is God waiting for e-mail prayer warriors to let God know what needs to be done? Does God count prayers to determine who gets thumbs-up or thumbs-down?

Laura grows so uncomfortable with sunshiny, pat answers that a couple of times she uses her illness as an excuse to hide at home.

Her family has conversations that stop when she walks into the room. One of the worst things about cancer is seeing it hurt the people she loves. She caught her husband watching a faith healer on television. He acted embarrassed, but if she had not walked in, would he have called the number at the bottom of the screen? A prayer cloth couldn't hurt.

She has never felt lonely before, but her friends treat her differently. People have stopped telling her their problems. She is no longer "Laura the one who does so much good work." Now she is "Laura who has cancer." A few of her friends are less likely to be there when she is not doing well.

One of her oncologists is the same way. When the news is bad, he looks as though he is disappointed with her, as though she failed treatment rather than the other way around, as though she is going to be a blemish on his scorecard. Her doctors—and she has enough to fill the Supreme Court—seem competent. They are comfortable talking about what radiation and chemotherapy might or might not do, but none of them are much help in telling her how to care for her children.

She hates her wig and is sick of throwing up. She has been mutilated, poisoned, and burned. She is angry when she is not depressed. When she wakes up in the morning, her first thought is, "I have cancer." God is a million miles away.

Her story could, of course, go another way. How different would Laura's story be if her faith and her church helped her deal with cancer honestly? Some Christians believe in an all-powerful God who chooses whom to heal and whom to punish, but there are also Christians who believe in an all-loving God who cares for and suffers with us all.

There are certainly people who prayed for healing and were healed, but there are also good people who prayed and died too soon. When you put these two sets of experiences together, you end up with hard questions. Were the prayers of those who prayed for healing and were healed more valid than the prayers of those who were not healed? That doesn't make sense. Maybe it's better to ask hard questions than it is to pretend to have all the answers.

The church should be a place to be real—to weep, pray, sing, and be silent in the face of sorrow. Whenever anyone hears the word "malignant," God's heart is the first to break. It is not God's will that anyone should die too soon. God is caring for us in every situation as much as God can, or else God is not God. God is not an all-controlling being who punishes us for unknown reasons. God is an all-compassionate being who shares in our suffering.

One of Laura's friends gives her a copy of a column by Molly Ivins, a breast cancer victim who writes, "I suspect that cancer doesn't give a rat's ass whether you have a positive mental attitude. The only reason to have a positive mental attitude is that it makes life better. It doesn't cure cancer."

Some of Laura's best friends are the ones who don't say anything at all. Silence is usually better than "You'll be fine."

Her friends call, and Laura is glad to talk to women who have been through cancer. She learns to speak with her family honestly concerning her fears about what may come. They help each other laugh. She loves her husband and children more passionately than before.

She makes her doctors tell the truth and tells them exactly what she wants and how they are going to help her get there.

Maybe it takes more faith to live with cancer than it does to be healed from cancer.

Laura and those who love her pray for healing that includes more than a return to normal health. Healing means patching up relationships, forgiving everyone including herself, and finding some peace. Healing is the Hebrew *shalom*, wholeness in the face of her illness, emotional healing, coping with grief, and being reconciled to herself, others, and God.

Prayer is not telling God what to do. It is the means by which Laura shares her heart with God. Prayer is being held in God's comfort, knowing that God is always working for our healing.

When we suffer, God suffers. When we hurt, God hurts. If we have cancer, then God has cancer. When we experience exhaustion, failure, and despair, God doesn't sympathize with our suffering from a safe distance; God shares it by entering our lives. The central truth of the cross is that God suffers with us.

Knowing that God goes through it with us doesn't take the sorrow away, but it offers hope beyond our grief. Even at our most frightened, God is with us. Laura's faith is in God who holds her in God's hands. Her faith is deeper and more meaningful than the faith she had before she became ill. It is nowhere near worth the cost, but she has a sense of being more and not less because of her illness. Some days she thinks her faith is growing faster than her cancer.

When she wakes up in the morning, sometimes her first thought is, "I have cancer," but then her second thought is, "I have today."

God is with her each day. God is her comfort, strength, and hope, caring for her and standing with her. The blessed bread, which is now broken, brings healing. The holy cup, poured out for all, is our salvation.

HOMEWARD BOUND

PSALM 84

How lovely is your dwelling place, O LORD of hosts! My soul longs, indeed it faints for the courts of the LORD . . . . (Psalm 84:1-2)

"I want to go home" is not just the plaintive cry of kindergarten students on the first day of school; it is the longing of every person who pays attention to his or her heart. For some, nothing is better than going home. Our memories of home grow sweeter as the years pass. Wherever we are never quite lives up to where we once were.

For others, going home is painful. We have scars that will not heal and memories we would like to forget. We hope that Thomas Wolfe is right, that we can't go home again, because home is the last place we want to go.

For most, home is both a blessing and a curse. Our memories are a source of comfort as well as anger, joy as well as sadness. We don't want to go home to stay, but we hope that home will always be there for us.

When people ask where I'm from, I say "Mississippi" gladly, because Mississippi is a nice place to be from. Much of what is Mississippi encourages mixed emotions: red clay, kudzu, Southern belles, steel magnolias, sweet potatoes, okra, Ole Miss, William Faulkner, Tennessee Williams, Brett Favre, "Boycott Disney" bumper stickers, "Don't Blame Me I Voted for Goldwater" bumper stickers, grocery stores with real names like "Piggly Wiggly" and "Jitney Jungle," gas stations where people ask, "Where you headed?" and then, "It won't take you an hour now that they've finished the highway" (which was finished in 1972). And then there's Elvis, who went to high school with my ninth grade biology teacher. She never forgave herself for not paying any attention to Elvis. More than once, Mrs. Stowers wondered aloud if she could have been the queen of Graceland.

When my family visits my parents, we stay in a house built on the farm my grandparents lived on for more than sixty years. What used to be a barn is east of the house. The wind patterns were not considered when they built the barn, a combination garage and cow stall. The car was parked on one side and the cows were milked on the other. Hay was in the loft over both sides. A big cooler kept the milk and watermelons a degree above frozen. My grandfather was good at milking. He could hit an open mouth from fifteen feet. He tried to teach me to milk, but I was never good at it. I'm not sure what that says about a person. When it was quiet, which was most of the time, the railing in that barn was as good a place to sit as I have ever sat.

My grandparents named several cows after their grandchildren—including one named "Brett." One evening at dinner, Grandpa asked how my hamburger tasted, and everyone at the table laughed. I didn't finish my meal after it was explained that I was what was for dinner.

The last time we went for a funeral, my family was welcomed by an assortment of saints and sinners who hugged me, hugged Carol, and hugged, kissed, and pinched the cheeks of my unprepared sons. A few hugged me before they asked who I was. When I answered, "I'm Clarice's oldest boy," they hugged me again.

Some of the conversations are in a foreign language I no longer understand: "Brett, we baled three thousand bales last year, round bales, not the little ones. Guess how many acres that took?"

I was lost.

"Take a guess."

"I really don't know."

"Just take a guess."

"Thirty?"

"Thirty?"

"Did I say thirty? I meant to say three hundred. Three thousand?"

Mississippi is a good place to call home because when the prodigals return, we hope that folks will recognize that we don't quite fit in. At the same time, we want to feel like we never left.

We want to go home to the home with the welcome mat on the porch and the home that we know only by its absence, home where there are dirty dishes in the sink and home that we have never even visited, home where the dog is not allowed on the couch and home where the deer and the antelope play, home sweet home, sweet home Alabama, your Old Kentucky home, home where the country roads take you, home where your homeboys hung long before you knew they were homeboys, where charity begins, where the home fires are burning, where the chickens come to roost, and where the angels are coming for to carry you. Be it ever so humble, there is no place like home. Even if it is the home we know only by our longing.

Three thousand years ago, the Hebrew people sang about longing for home. About twenty of the psalms are traveling songs sung to lift people's spirits and to pass the time as worshipers made their way to the temple. Psalm 84 was their version of "one hundred bottles of beer on the wall."

They sang, "God, what a lovely home, you have. No place is as gorgeous as any place where you dwell."

They felt most at home in the temple with its feasting, dancing, and celebrating. The Israelites sang that one day at home with God is better than a thousand on the beaches of a Greek island.

"O God, you are our home," they sang. "We long to be at home with you. Like swallows and sparrows yearn for a nest, we hope for a shelter, a refuge, a home with God."

We understand this longing. We have restless hearts. Something is unfinished in us. Sometimes we feel like we're not at home in our hometown, our family, even our own skin. Our stories are the search for a home we have never seen, for a marvelous reality just out of reach.

Though it doesn't seem like it, the homesickness we feel is a gift of God, because it helps us recognize the occasional, obscure glimpses of home. C. S. Lewis wrote,

The sweetest thing in all my life has been the longing to find the place where all the beauty came from . . . . At present we are on the outside of the world, the wrong side of the door. We discern the freshness and purity of morning, but they do not make us fresh and pure. We cannot mingle with the splendors we see. But all the leaves of the New Testament are rustling with the rumor that it will not always be so. Someday, God willing, we shall get in. (Deborah Smith Douglas, "C. S. Lewis and Our Longing for Home" *Weavings* [July/August 2000]: 11, 16)

Every once in a while, for just a moment, we come close to finding our home far away. Our search for home leads us to blessed people, holy places, and sacred moments, when we are with the people we love, when we glimpse home in the goodness of others, when we are alone listening to the silence, and when we close our eyes and feel God's welcoming grace and give ourselves again to hope.

The home for which our weary hearts long is God. Nothing else will make us feel completely at home. Someday our longing for home will be satisfied. We will be safely and forever at home with God.

Jesus, who spent his life homesick for God, set the table. Ours is a pilgrim existence, but by faith we travel hopefully, wander confidently, let go of where we are in favor of where we can go, welcome others on the journey, eat the bread of life, and drink the cup of grace, understanding that the table celebrates our eternal home with God.

ALL YOU NEED

MATTHEW 14:13-21

Taking the five loaves and the two fish, Jesus looked up to heaven, and blessed and broke the loaves, and gave them to the disciples, and the disciples gave them to the crowds. And all ate and were filled. (Matthew 14:19-20)

Each morning Monday through Friday, about 125 people line up on the west side of the church. At 9:00, church members start handing out sack lunches—Vienna sausages, chips, a granola bar, sometimes a fruit cup, and a Bible verse. We call it a sack lunch, but at 9:15, people are sitting on the sidewalk eating their lunch for breakfast because they are hungry.

About 120 families a month come for groceries. Church members smile as they hand out sacks for our guests to fill with crackers, tuna, beans, corn, peas, soup, rice, and cereal. Our neighbors often look embarrassed to be asking for food, but they are hungry. Sometimes they open the corn flakes on the way home.

On Thursday nights, the line starts forming long before we open the doors. At 6:00, about 200 guests come inside for a good meal. After dinner there is a worship service, but not everyone stays. That's fine. They come because they are hungry.

One Thursday night as we are finishing the meal, Cliff asks, "Can I play your piano?"

I answer, "Only if you're good."

He smiles as he says, "I'm not any good."

He is lying. He opens with "Crying" by Roy Orbison. Then "Alone Again (Naturally)" by Gilbert O'Sullivan, then a Righteous Brothers song. Everybody at our table is playing "Name that Tune," but we can't come up with "Unchained Melody." Then "Heartbreak Hotel." Every song is about a heart breaking, but Cliff plays with such joy that you don't know whether to cry or laugh. He plays the notes and the notes between the notes.

What do you think the piano was thinking? That piano loves playing "The Old Rugged Cross" on Sunday mornings, but Elvis is good for the soul, too.

Carol wonders aloud, "Do you think Cliff plays requests?"

I hand her a dollar. Carol asks for "You Don't Know Me" by Ray Charles and gets a Ray Charles medley—"Georgia on My Mind," "What'd I Say," "I Can't Stop Loving You." It is the best dollar I have spent in a long time. I should have asked my wife to dance. I didn't because I can't dance, but there's no way we would have been the only ones.

Everyone is having so much fun. Cliff finishes. We applaud. He starts to leave, but Eddie, who came in late, shouts, "You can't quit yet. I haven't finished eating."

Cliff goes back to the piano for an encore and plays a version of "In the Mood" that would have made Glenn Miller green with envy. We are obviously hungry for something beyond the food we share.

Ten thousand people are following Jesus. His compassion is the magnet that draws a huge crowd of hurting people to a lonely beach. Jesus heals and teaches them, but as it gets on toward evening, the disciples say, "It's great that you helped all these people, but it's after 5:00. It's quitting time. You need to send them on their way."

Jesus surprises them. "They don't need to leave. You can feed them. What have you got?"

The disciples are incredulous. "Look at how many people are here. All we have are five lousy pieces of bread and two fish. What good is that going to do?"

Jesus blesses the loaves and fish, breaks it, and gives it to the disciples to give to the congregation. The crackers and tuna become Babette's feast, Thanksgiving at Plymouth Rock, Christmas at Tiny

Tim's, dinner at Joe T. Garcia's, all you can eat at Ruth's Chris Steakhouse, the feast of Ramadan, a Moravian love feast, a Hawaiian luau, and an unlocked Ben and Jerry's.

This is more than a story of free fast food. Even the people who are there are not sure exactly what happened.

Every once in a while at a church picnic, you hear, "We're almost out of bread. What are we going to do?"

Someone who is not as funny as he thinks responds, "The pastor's here. Give him a couple of loaves and let him take it from there."

That's what we do with this story—see it as a magic trick, laugh it off, or try to come up with a rational explanation. One theory is that the crowd was motivated by the generosity of the disciples to share food they had tucked away for themselves. The point of the story is the importance of sharing.

But this story is not about magic or a sweet little lesson. The Good Samaritan, the prodigal son, the water into wine, the woman at the well, Mary and Martha, and the raising of Lazarus—those stories only make it into one Gospel. This story about Jesus feeding the crowd is one of only a few that are recorded in all four Gospels.

The church told and retold this story. They believed we would need to hear it. This miracle that happened once in "a lonely place" became a story that happens again and again in a million places.

In John's version, Jesus says, "I am the bread of life, and the one who comes to me will not hunger." Notice the words Matthew uses: Jesus took the loaves, blessed, broke, and gave them to the disciples. The verbs "take," "bless," "break," and "give" are the same words in the same order as those used to describe his actions at the Last Supper.

This is Communion. Jesus offers hungry people more than food. He invites us to the Lord's Table. If we were not hungry, then not only would drive-thru restaurants be out of business, but so would the writers of self-help books, plastic surgeons, Lexus dealers, computer dating services, and the Lottery Commission.

Many of us know the feeling of a midlife crisis that shows up early and stays late. We are standing in front of the refrigerator, knowing we want something but not sure what it is.

Are we hungry for faith? Hope? Love? A sense of belonging? God? We have heard a rumor of a God who feeds the hungry and fills the soul. Our hunger leads us to the table, the promise of home, the heavenly banquet.

Far more than 5,000 come to the table each day. Around the world, hungry people share the gift. In the bread and cup, God gives strength because we get discouraged. God gives grace because we do not always feel accepted. God gives generosity because we get used to thinking only of ourselves. God gives love because we desperately want to be loved. At the table, we taste the goodness of a day when there will be no more longing.

THE PHARISEE IN US

MATTHEW 23:1-12

*The Pharisees do all their deeds to be seen by others; for
they make their phylacteries broad and their fringes long.
They love to have the place of honor at banquets and the
best seats in the synagogues. (Matthew 23:5-6)*

I tacked this quotation to the bulletin board in my office: "You
have reached the pinnacle of success as soon as you become
uninterested in money, compliments, or publicity." After a few days,
I took it down. By O. A. Battista's criteria, most of us are still some
distance from the pinnacle of success.

Jesus walks into Jerusalem with his disciples tired from the trip,
but a crowd begins to form. He points to the back of the crowd where
he sees an elderly man looking for a place to sit. Jesus motions for the
man to come up front and sit with him.

Jesus starts talking with a widow who is still wearing her funeral
clothes. She has been crying for months. Everyone has heard her sad
story too many times, but Jesus listens.

A small child with big brown eyes waves her arms for Jesus to hold
her. One of the disciples tries to stop her, but Jesus picks up the little
girl. Jesus looks into the eyes of each person as though he knows them
personally.

He notices a group standing to the side wearing phylacteries and
long tassels. The fringes are used like a rosary. Phylacteries are leather
boxes containing portions of Scripture that are worn on the forehead.
The outfits make it clear that the wearers are religious.

Jesus begins, "All of us need to take seriously the directions of scripture."

The Old Testament professors like that part, but Jesus says, "Especially the scribes and Pharisees. They don't get it. They expect everyone else to live up to a carefully selected set of rules—the ones they find easy to follow and others find hard. Don't be like them. Don't see yourself as more important than others. Don't see your sisters and brothers as problems to be solved or tools to be used to your advantage. Those who promote themselves will be humbled. All who humble themselves will be promoted. The least, last, and lost are first, most, and found in the kingdom."

Writing about this story is difficult for any minister who loves to wear fringe. I love donning my pulpit robe and stoles and marching in processionals. I have no doubt that Jesus is talking about me. Jesus may be talking about you.

The Pharisee in us judges others by their shortcomings. We weed out the people we like from the people we do not. Whenever someone fails to treat us as we think we should be treated, we mark that person off the list.

Like the Pharisees, we want people to think we are better than we are. We like to be admired. Like a millionaire football player strutting in the end zone after a touchdown, when we do something good we pause a moment so everyone can see who it was. Who doesn't enjoy giving orders more than taking them? Would we rather sit at the head table or wash dishes afterward?

Servanthood may not be attractive to us, but it is to Jesus. Christ inverts the pyramid. Jesus tells his followers not to have the prevailing attitudes of teachers, parents, and leaders. All who exalt themselves will be humbled. All who humble themselves will be exalted.

One of our difficulties in learning not to seek status is that, at first glance, Jesus appears to be offering a new hierarchy. Even this paradoxical "whoever humbles themselves will be exalted" can be used as a ladder by status seekers. Everything we do—even trying to be humble—becomes a means of self-exaltation.

A rabbi rushed to the altar, fell to his knees, and cried, "I'm nobody! I'm nobody!"

The cantor of the synagogue, impressed by this example of humility, joined the rabbi on his knees, saying, "I'm nobody. I'm nobody!"

The custodian, watching from the corner, could not restrain himself either. He joined the other two on his knees, calling out, "I'm nobody! I'm nobody!"

At that point the rabbi, nudging the cantor with his elbow, pointed at the custodian and said, "Look who thinks he's nobody!"

If we are ever truly humble, it will not happen by an act of will. Our motivations will never be completely pure. We need to see Jesus' motivation for calling us to service. Christ tells us to serve because Christ understands that blessing takes place in the midst of service. We can pass on our fifteen minutes of fame because service leads to joy.

The humility that Jesus demands will not come because we forget ourselves. Humility happens as we remember others, as we discover that we are in this together. We should not define ourselves as superior or inferior. We should define ourselves by the grace of God. We do not have to impress each other with our wisdom or our humility in order to have a place at Christ's table.

The recognition for which we yearn is a gift of God. To have one gracious God means that we are children of the same family. To have one teacher means that we are all students. To have one master means that we are servants together. Over against our hierarchies, Jesus proposes a radical egalitarianism. The grace of God covers parents and children, teachers and students, even scribes and Pharisees. Karl Barth said, "Nowhere is the grace of God more evident than in the fact that some preachers will be saved"—even ones who love marching in the processional.

As the service draws to a close, people move into the aisle. One man starts to get in line, and he sees an elderly man who is always talking about his problems. He usually avoids the old guy for fear that he will get an earful of the man's latest difficulties, but the line for Communion should be a safe place. He looks around at the others waiting. He sees a woman who disagrees with him on an issue he thinks is important. He does not think much of her. His mind wanders. He wonders why the other line always moves faster. If this self-absorbed man ever loved the people around him, he has forgotten.

Several spots behind the Pharisee is a woman who also notices the elderly man with the long list of problems. She tells herself that the next time he wants to talk, she will be more patient. She thinks about the words of Christ: "The greatest among you will be your servant." She asks God to help her live with a servant's heart and give herself to the people around her. She realizes that she has been blessed. When she looks into the eyes of the people with whom she shares Communion, she gives thanks. If we come to the table with sisters and brothers and feel no jealousy, it is a gift of God's grace. We take the supper as God's children.

Caring for Country

MATTHEW 25:14-30

For to all those who have, more will be given, and they will have an abundance; but from those who have nothing, even what they have will be taken away. As for this worthless slave, throw him into the outer darkness, where there will be weeping and gnashing of teeth. (Matthew 25:29-30)

Even standing in line at the National Archives is inspiring. The original Declaration of Independence is on the left: "We hold these truths to be self-evident, that all men are created equal, that they are endowed by their creator with certain inalienable rights, among these are life, liberty and the pursuit of happiness . . . . That to secure these rights, governments are instituted among men, deriving their just powers from the consent of the governed."

That declaration was a blowtorch that lit up the world. No one had ever said in such a glorious way that people have a right to rule themselves. The rich and poor have equal standing. We forget how stunning it was.

The Constitution, in the center, is the longest lasting written constitution in the world. The founding fathers rejected the idea of property qualifications for holding office because they wanted no part of "veneration for wealth." Their goal was to preserve equal opportunities by destroying any alliance between government and money.

The Bill of Rights may be even more amazing: "Congress shall make no law respecting an establishment of religion, or prohibiting the free exercise thereof; or abridging the freedom of speech, or of the press; or of the right of the people peaceably to assemble, and to petition the government for a redress of grievances."

The first amendment puts every citizen on the same footing. Page Smith reminds us, "Their ambition was not merely to free themselves from dependence and subordination to the crown, but to inspire people everywhere to create agencies of government and forms of common social life that would offer greater dignity and hope to the exploited and suppressed."

Carol and I were following a father and daughter around the rotunda. We heard the father whisper, "This is the Bill of Rights. It says that every person is free."

The little girl stared at that aging, fading document and said, "It looks like it's falling apart."

To which her father replied, "It's been through a lot."

Our country has been through a lot—much of it hard and much of it wonderful. We have been given great blessings and responsibility. Where do you think the United States is in Jesus' story?

Just before going overseas for a year, a rich executive calls three employees in and says, "I'm going to give you a chance to prove yourselves. I'm leaving some money for you to work with. When I come back, I expect a profit."

He gives the first $500,000, the second $200,000, the third $100,000. The year passes quickly. The first two take chances with what they have been given and do well. The owner calls them "good and faithful" and invites them to dinner with him. The third is lazy and selfish. He hoards what he's been given, hiding the money where no one can get to it. What he doesn't understand is that the money was never his to keep. The executive says, "Throw him into the outer darkness where there will be weeping and gnashing of teeth." This harsh story is a warning to those who think that they've done their duty in merely keeping what they've been given.

The United States is a five-talent country. We have welcomed tired, poor, huddled masses. We have led the world in providing schools for children and care for the elderly. We have made progress in giving justice to all. Our country has in many ways lived out the goodness of her core values. We have been blessed and been a blessing.

We are a five-talent nation, but we are always tempted to act like a one-talent people, to hoard what we've been given. Government too easily falls into the hands of those who favor the haves over the have-nots.

That is why the gap between rich and poor is greater than it has been in fifty years—the worst inequality among western nations. Poverty is showing up where we haven't expected it—among families that include two parents who work. These newly poor are people who love their children and work hard to care for them. Although they are running hard, they keep falling farther behind.

The gap between them and prosperous America is widening. More children are growing up in poverty in our country than in any other industrial nation. Millions of workers are making less money today in real dollars than they did twenty years ago. Working people are putting in longer hours just to stay in place. The Republicans and Democrats argue over who is the real champion of the middle class. Neither seems to care about those with the greatest needs.

Franklin Roosevelt said, "The test of our progress is not whether we add more to the abundance of those who have much; it is whether we provide enough for those who have little."

The poverty that persists amid great wealth, the growing gap between the rich and poor, and the maldistribution of wealth and opportunity should break our hearts.

Since he won the Nobel Peace Prize, Jimmy Carter has been asked many times to identify the greatest threat to peace. He says the greatest danger is "the growing chasm between the haves and have-nots—a gap that contributes to oppression, injustice, hunger, disease and war."

Jesus lived with compassion for the poor and forgotten. Christ's followers live with the same compassion. God wants us to bless America, to make our country more caring. So Christians do not vote to support their own pocketbooks but to help people whose pocketbooks are empty.

We raise our voices for those who don't get heard. We work to provide low-income housing, improve schools, expand job opportunities, promote financial security in retirement, support the mentally ill, and offer assistance for the working poor.

We ask hard questions about our government's policies. Do they represent the common good of society rather than the interests of an elite few? Do they show sensitivity to the spirit of the golden rule? Do they refrain from the arrogant assumption that the powerful have the right to ignore the needs of the hurting? Do they widen the gap between rich and poor?

Christ's followers know that the less fortunate are sisters and brothers. We take Christ's example seriously. Bill Moyers wrote,

> Over the past few years, as the poor got poorer, the health care crisis worsened, wealth became more and more concentrated, and our political system was bought out from under us, prophetic Christianity lost its voice. The religious right drowned everyone else out. And they hijacked Jesus. The very Jesus who stood in Nazareth and proclaimed, "The Lord has anointed me to preach the good news to the poor." The very Jesus who challenged the religious orthodoxy of the day by feeding the hungry on the Sabbath, who offered kindness to the prostitute and hospitality to the outcast, who said the kingdom of heaven belongs to little children, raised the status of women, and treated even the tax collector like a child of God. This Jesus has been hijacked and turned into a guardian of privilege instead of a champion of the dispossessed. Let's get Jesus back. (Bill Moyers, "Call to Renewal," keynote address, Washington, D.C., 24 May 2004)

Caring for the poor is not a partisan issue. It doesn't matter if you're a liberal or a conservative; Jesus is both and neither. It doesn't matter if you're a Democrat or a Republican—Jesus is both and neither. God calls us all to become more like Christ by caring for the hurting.

God invites to the table those who are given to grace, who help those who are hurting, and who seek God's mercy. Sharing the supper is promising to live as Christ's followers.

Honest to God

Mark 7:1-8, 14-15, 21-23

So the Pharisees and the scribes asked Jesus, "Why do your disciples not live according to the tradition of the elders, but eat with defiled hands?" (Mark 7:5)

You probably don't need me to write about *Miss Manners' Guide to Excruciatingly Correct Behavior*. You may have read it several times. Perhaps you have underlined portions for your children or spouse. We love Miss Manners' strong opinions.

If you have not sent a thank-you letter for any gift you received more than thirty minutes ago, Miss Manners has no mercy on you. You are also in trouble if you sent your thank-you via e-mail, Facebook, or Twitter. There is, in Miss Manners' world, no such thing as a thank-you *note*. You must begin your thank-you *letter* with a "burst of enthusiasm" and make sure it "names the present with a flattering adjective."

The *only* excuse for declining an invitation to be a pallbearer is "a plan to have one's own funeral in the near future."

Do not wear black to a wedding. If you are in deep mourning, you should not come in the first place.

Even the young are expected to act with extreme manners. When a six-year-old reader asks what is important enough to tell his mother when she is talking to company, Miss Manners provides a short list that includes "Mommy, the kitchen is full of smoke."

Good rules come in handy. They help things go smoothly. What would Judith Martin include if she decided to write *Miss Manners' Guide to Excruciatingly Correct Church Behavior?*

Be on time for worship. This means *before* the music begins. The first note is not a starter's pistol for the hundred-yard dash.

Children need to learn the sacred nature of worship. This means no chewing gum, iPods, or iPhones. Stare with disdain at anyone whose cell phone rings.

Try not to draw attention to yourself by singing louder than any three people on your row. The only satisfactory excuses for *not* singing are life-threatening conditions.

When faced with the question of what is important enough to whisper to the gentle worshiper seated next to you, it must be as crucial as "Mommy, the sanctuary is full of smoke."

When speaking to the preacher after worship, begin with a "burst of enthusiasm" and "a flattering adjective" in relation to the sermon.

After a particularly offensive sermon, use an exit other than the one where the preacher is standing.

Miss Manners is the patron saint of the Pharisees. They share her belief that manners hold everything together. On this occasion they see Jesus' disciples displaying terrible manners and ignoring tradition by eating without first ceremonially washing their hands. The book of Leviticus—and Miss Manners would agree with this—insists that priests dip their hands in water before they eat. The Pharisees reason that if priests need to be holy, then everyone else should be holy, too.

Jesus' disciples are from the back woods of Galilee, where people aren't so formal. Fishermen who have their hands in water all the time don't bother with ceremonies. None of the disciples need a fork at Bojangles.

The Pharisees ask, "Why won't Jesus keep the rules about the Sabbath? Why does he hang around with such an ill-mannered crowd?"

Understanding their frustration is easy. How would you feel if you invited Jesus and some church friends to your house for a fancy Sunday lunch, and when you ask Jesus to say the blessing he replies, "No, let's just dig in"?

We know our religious traditions as well as the Pharisees knew theirs. We know what to expect at church. We know when to sit, when to stand, and when we are not expected to pay attention.

We know what's expected of good church people outside the church. We know the words to say and the words to avoid in certain company. We know what we're supposed to do and what church people aren't to be seen doing. Like the Pharisees, we have learned how to judge others by how well they follow our rules.

Christianity has created expectations that have little to do with Jesus' teachings. Throughout church history, the majority of Christians have advocated ethics more like the Pharisees' than like Jesus'. We know how to mind our manners.

Most of the traditions are okay. There is nothing wrong with the Pharisees washing their hands. Parents would love for their children to be more like Pharisees when it comes to ritual cleanliness. The mistake lies in turning a helpful ritual into a judgment. Common people in Palestine had little access to clean water. Going through this ceremony three times a day would have been difficult and meaningless. Going through the motions to appear religious is more dangerous than it first appears because pretense becomes second nature.

Looking like we are worshiping is easier than listening to God, singing the melodies is easier than hearing the words, and attending church is easier than giving ourselves to God.

The church, at its worst, is a gathering of people who want to think of themselves as the kind of people who go to church. We get used to *acting* concerned, *behaving* like a friend, and *sounding* kind. We end up more concerned about our reputations than our souls. The more attention we give to outward appearances, the less we give to our hearts.

Harriet Beecher Stowe wrote that she went to a party where everyone seemed to have left themselves at home. Church can feel like everyone left themselves at home. We treat one another as though we are in-laws meeting for the first time and trying to make a good impression. The church of the Pharisees is a collection of performers acting like church people should act.

If our hearts belong to God, nothing else is needed, and if our hearts are not God's, then nothing else matters. Masquerading as anything other than what we are destroys us from the inside.

Pretending to be something we aren't is deadly. We waste our lives asking, "How do I look? What do people think of me?"

Jesus tries to make it clear: "What can be seen is not what matters. What's in your heart is what matters. What's inside keeps us from life."

In Frederick Buechner's *The Book of Bebb*, Antonio Parr speaks of meeting the woman he loves: "I wanted to open my heart to [her] not so much so she could see what was inside, but so I could" (New York: Atheneum, 1979).

In opening our hearts to God, we learn what is inside. We have to choose to see the evil that lurks within us. If we are honest with God, we have to admit hard truths: we ignore God; we waste good gifts; we fail to be true to our own standards; we are blind to the suffering of others; we have a lack of concern for the wrongs that do not touch us and are over-sensitive to the wrongs that do.

In the Gospel of Thomas, which did not make it into the Bible, Jesus says, "If you bring forth what's inside you, what you bring forth will save you. If you don't bring forth what's inside you, what you bring forth can destroy you."

With God's help, we live authentically. We open the depths of our souls to God's grace. We move beyond old habits to a more genuine way.

As God leads us to new life, God brings life to our old traditions. Worship becomes a means by which God touches our hearts. The stories of faith become an avenue by which we hear God's voice. The best rules become directions to the good life.

God delivers us from the tyranny of tired hypocrisy. Lives spent trying to look good pale in comparison to lives given to God. We don't need to impersonate caring people; we can love. We don't need to judge ourselves by what others think; we can live out God's grace. We don't need to be insincere; we can be real. We don't need to go through the motions of the Lord's Supper; we can come to the table and give ourselves to God.

AM I AT THE RIGHT TABLE?

LUKE 14:1, 7-14

"But when you give a banquet, invite those who are poor and maimed and lame and blind, and you will be blessed, because they cannot repay you, for you will be repaid at the resurrection of the righteous." (Luke 14:13-14)

Phoebe Reese is delighted to find out that she's been chosen for a special task force on community economic development. After working as an assistant professor at Texas Christian University for five years, she was starting to wonder about tenure. So much of her work had centered on Fort Worth's economy that she'd worried about being able to get a job anywhere else. Being chosen for the task force is a sign that associate professor status is on the way.

When the system works against you, it's miserable, but when it works for you, you remember how much fun it is to be at the head of the class. The ladder looks most evil from the bottom rung.

The stated purpose of the task force is to decide how to spend a government grant to attract computer industries to large cities in Texas. The real goal is for Fort Worth to gain some of the high-paying jobs that Austin's budding Silicon Valley usually takes. Phoebe has doubts about the success of this venture, but she plans to keep her doubts to herself.

The first meeting is an informal get-acquainted luncheon. As Phoebe arrives, the chair of the committee walks over and offers an apology that he will repeat for everyone at the meeting: "I'm sorry about the restaurant. We chose it because it was quick and easy to get to. I know that the atmosphere isn't what we're used to, but I'm sure we'll have a fine meal—even if it's plain."

The table is filled with movers and shakers: the director of Economic Development; the city manager; the chair of the economics department at TCU; the president of the Chamber of Commerce; a state representative; two city council members; an assortment of lawyers in Armani suits. Phoebe doesn't know two women at the other end of the table but suspects that they're consultants from a high-powered public relations firm. The mayor comes in late, and everybody has to move down a seat so that he can have a prime spot. There are no place cards at the table, but there is a definite pecking order.

Phoebe thinks that this is the most important group of people with whom she has ever eaten. Everyone at the table is well educated, with good teeth and no dirt under their fingernails. She can hardly keep from looking at the door to see who is coming in next.

Phoebe had to work hard for her place at the table. Her parents were not able to help much, but they are proud of her. Every year in the family Christmas letter, her mother brags about her daughter with the Ph.D. who teaches at Texas Christian University. Her mother always emphasizes the "Christian" part. A copy of her dissertation is on her parents' mantle. Her father has never read it, but he loves to tell people the title: "The Application of Bayesian Methods for Estimating the Effects of Capital Improvement Projects on the Economic Performance of Medium Sized Cities." It does roll off the tongue.

Phoebe hopes that someone she knows will walk by and see her sitting with these important people. She tries to be herself, but she can't stop thinking, "How am I doing? Do I sound smart?" She wishes that she had taken etiquette lessons or read Emily Post. Eating in front of people you want to impress is awkward.

Phoebe notices a table in a glassed-off area in the corner of the room. Outside she had seen a Lexus parked next to a Ford Pinto next to a BMW next to the world's largest collection of rust. Now it makes sense.

A woman at the table is still wearing her white hair net. She works in the kitchen. She must have invited the people at her table. The teenager seated next to her may be her son. His eyes are bloodshot, and his nose is running. A smiling woman in a doctor's outfit works at a clinic near Stop Six. She used to give speeches on public health issues, but then people found out that she performs abortions and many stopped inviting her. Phoebe thinks she might have seen one of the people at the table at the corner of Lancaster and Jennings. A sign lying on the floor by his chair says, "Iraq Vet, Will Work for Food." A white-haired Asian couple is speaking something other than English. The man may have Alzheimer's. A girl in a tank top is feeding two small children. She is not wearing a wedding ring.

The people at the table in the corner are eating more and speaking louder than those at the table in the center. These two groups of people in the same room provide quite a contrast. Peace in the Middle East is more probable than these two groups pushing their tables together and bringing in more chairs.

Phoebe realizes that seated at the end of the corner table is a friend she has not seen since high school. Jessie is one of the few African-American friends Phoebe has had. Jessie is asking the veteran to "Hand her a roll, please" and offering the doctor a second cup of coffee. Now she's putting jelly on toast for the mother of two and trying to make one of the babies smile.

After graduating from college, Jessie disappointed her parents and teachers by deciding not to get a master's degree. She took a job with social services. That must be how she knows these people. Jessie sits in the middle of the group, laughing loudly as if everything is just fine.

Where is the waitress with the iced tea? Good waitresses recognize which tables are going to leave the best tips.

Phoebe carefully wipes the corner of her mouth with her napkin and ponders the dichotomy in the room. She and Jessie were friends. They grew up in the same neighborhood. How could they live in such different worlds now? What makes someone the kind of person Jessie obviously is? Could Phoebe have been like her? Would she want to?

As Jessie cuts the Asian gentleman's meat, Phoebe asks herself, "How do you become comfortable around people who make you uncomfortable?"

Can it be natural to choose friends on the basis of what they need rather than what they can give you? Doesn't it get tiresome caring for people who can't do anything for you? Could a brilliant young economist think about supply and need as well as supply and demand without it getting in the way of her career?

Is it even possible to treat a child as though she is as important as a senator? Is it foolish to think an autistic person matters as much as a university professor? Do we really want to see value in every person?

The Iraq veteran is getting more strawberry shortcake for the young mother. He walks with a limp. The corporate executive sitting next to Phoebe notices that she is staring at the corner table and says, "This isn't exactly the Ritz."

Then something Phoebe had hoped would not happen does. Jessie catches Phoebe's eye. A spark of recognition and a big grin break out on Jessie's face. She walks toward Phoebe's table. What should happen next? Should Phoebe introduce Jessie to the people at her table? What if Jessie wants to introduce her friends to Phoebe? What will she do? Is she supposed to feel bad for eating with important people? Is it her fault that some people don't fit some situations? Are there tables where everyone is welcome?

You're Already
on the Team

1 Timothy 1:12-17

The saying is sure and worthy of full acceptance,
that Christ Jesus came into the world to save sinners.
(1 Timothy 1:15)

The air in the middle school gym is thick with the smell of yesterday's heroes, the squeak of tennis shoes, and pressure more intense than any Final Four. The sign over the bathroom has it right: "Through these doors walk champions." Ten-year-olds, concerned parents, and unconcerned siblings gather for the excruciating experience of tryouts.

The coach in charge is nice, but one of the other coaches looks too much like Rick Pitino. Warm-ups consist primarily of players watching each other warm up while pretending not to. Several are fascinated with the bottoms of their Nikes—which cost more than your first car. Some chatter nervously: "I think I should have played soccer." And some trash talk: "His mother made him wear long pants."

A player in a San Antonio Spurs jersey looks older than most fifth graders. He is about my height—which is not impressive unless you are ten—and he has a moustache.

The anxiety increases as they begin with layups. The first future LeBron James or Dirk Nowitzki throws up a brick and looks like he might cry. The second NBA prospect forgets to dribble. Several look surprised by the shape of the ball and the height of the hoop.

The free throws are painful to watch. They shoot a Shaq-like percentage. The line seems forty feet from the goal, but, and I should not write this, my son Caleb hit two of three.

The coach tells his all-stars to dribble to mid-court and back. This leads to the question, "What's mid-court?"

To his credit, the coach keeps saying things like "good try" and "almost."

He tries to encourage them, but they are too nervous to hear. Every missed shot brings a painful grimace from the shooter and his parents, and a look of relief on every other player's face.

They know that bad things could happen. The ball could hit you, you could dribble off your foot, or you could miss a shot and hear your little brother yell, "Airball!"

Most of the players look like they wish they were somewhere else.

We know what tryouts feel like. Some days it seems like we will never get past the fear of kicking the ball out of bounds. We imagine people with clipboards making a list of our mistakes.

We spend too much time trying to look good. We want people to think we are important. We want to achieve things that would impress our parents. We are still trying to make A's, even though no one is filling out report cards.

When we try to be who we think others think we should be, we end up living someone else's life. Yet we keep trying to impress people. Maybe we are trying to impress ourselves.

No one worked harder to impress the coaches than Paul. He really thought that he was trying out for God's team. Paul worked hard as a Pharisee, standing up for what he had been taught, fighting the infidels.

But that was years ago. Now Paul is trying to encourage his young friend in a new pastorate at First Christian Church, Ephesus. If, as some scholars suggest, Paul didn't write First Timothy, then someone who'd been reading Paul's diary did.

Paul and Timothy have been good for one another. Paul has been a spiritual mentor. They've gone on mission trips together. Paul sees Timothy as a long-term investment in the gospel.

Paul writes, "I'm so grateful to Jesus for inviting me to serve. He went out on a limb when he trusted me. The only credentials I had were self-righteousness, hatred, and arrogance."

Paul is not exaggerating. As "Saul," he was captain of the Pharisee storm troopers. The book of Acts says that Saul "breathed threats and murder against the disciples." He entered house after house, dragging off Christians and taking them to prison.

When Paul-as-Saul began persecuting the followers of Jesus, he thought he was doing the right thing. Many people who attack the defenseless believe they are advancing some cause. No one seems farther from the hopes God has for us than rampaging fanatics, sponsors of terrorism who breathe threats and murder and yet believe they are acting righteously. There is an old saying: "It ain't what I don't know that gets me in trouble, but what I know for sure that ain't so."

Saul was sure of himself. He was in charge of a goon squad going to Damascus to round up some trouble-making Christians when it happened. He was knocked flat by a blaze of light that made the sun look like a forty-watt bulb, and out of the light came a voice that called his name: "Saul, why are you out to get me?"

When he pulled himself together enough to ask, "Who wants to know?" to his horror, the response was, "I'm Jesus of Nazareth."

Saul waited for the axe to fall, but Jesus changed Saul's name and said, "You're on my team now."

Paul never forgot the joy and astonishment of that moment of grace.

As he writes Timothy, Paul reaches for the grandest language he can find: "the grace of God overflowed with faith and love." Desiring a loan for a hundred dollars, he received a check for ten million. Hoping for a stay of execution, he received a full pardon. Desiring a slice of bread, he was given the title to a Dunkin' Donuts.

Paul continues, "More than anything else, this is what I'm sure of: Jesus Christ came into the world to save, to show us the way, to reveal God's goodness. I'm proof—Public Sinner Number One, exhibit A of the grace of God."

Paul is beside himself with gratitude. Like in a Broadway musical, he breaks out in this ancient doxology: "Deep honor and bright glory to the King of All Time—One God, Immortal, Invisible, will hold us in love forever."

What does Paul tell his young friend is most important? Paul says that faith doesn't begin with our capabilities; it begins with God's grace. It doesn't matter how smart Timothy is or what he has accomplished. What matters is that God gives him the grace he needs more than anything else.

The hope for Christians is not that we'll do what's right; our hope is God loving us no matter what. Sometimes we don't feel like we have much to recommend us to God. The good news is that we don't need anything to recommend us to God. When we act as if the Lamb's Book of Life includes our resumes, we need to remember that the only things listed in the Lamb's Book of Life are our names.

When will we quit trying out? When will we stop wondering if we are going to make the team? How long will we feel like we are three inches too short? We spend too much of ourselves worrying about whether we are good enough. We may be weak on left-handed layups. The free-throw line may always be too far from the basket. But tryouts are done and God has chosen us. All that is left is for us to share the bread of God's mercy.

Supper at the Homesick Restaurant

Psalm 137

By the rivers of Babylon—
there we sat down and there we wept
when we remembered Zion. (Psalm 137:1)

My family moved a lot when I was growing up, so I have trouble remembering a particular house well—except for my grandparents' home in Mantachie, Mississippi. They never moved. In 1930, my grandfather, Guy Graham, hired a builder to construct a house on a corner of his in-laws' farm. Ten neighbors volunteered to help. They cut down trees my great-grandfather had planted and built a three-bedroom house that felt like home the minute you walked in the door. In my memories, the house is filled with laughter.

My heart broke when the house burned down. Lanny Harris, a volunteer fireman returning from a 911 medical call, saw smoke about 2:00 a.m. He kicked open the front door and woke the family who rented the house from my cousin for $400 a month. Five community fire departments were called, but the house was completely destroyed. The mother, a home health-care nurse, told reporters that it must have been old wiring, but my mother suspects that they left the propane heater on in the back because it was so cold that night. My grandparents never kept that heater on.

I know it was just a house, but I also know it was more than that. Remembering what is lost is painful. Most of us have memories that make us sad when we think of what is gone forever. Church is like that, with good memories that lead to sorrow.

Some mistakenly think that church should always be a party. Church is a place to wear your best clothes and think happy thoughts, because as someone said, the biggest religions in America are optimism and denial. Emily Dickinson could have been talking about shallow church when she wrote, "Pain—is missed—in Praise." Sometimes churches give the impression that when your life is falling apart, all you need to do is sing a happy song and pretend everything is fine.

When someone says, "I'm too depressed to go to church," it's a judgment on the church. No one should have to pretend in church. Worship that doesn't take sorrow seriously is not the worship of God.

The Israelites know how to bring their sorrows to God. By the rivers of Babylon, the Hebrew people sit down and weep. A terrible empire has overwhelmed this small group and taken everything they loved. They are haunted by the memories of their homes burned and their synagogues destroyed.

They come to the river looking for a quiet place. They bring their instruments, but they can't bring themselves to sing. The Babylonians taunt their slaves by asking them to sing one of the old, happy songs. But how can they sing "The Eyes of Texas" when they have been marched against their will to Idaho?

Grief turns into bitterness. They can't sing, but they won't forget the song: "If I should forget Jerusalem, let my hand that will not play the harp fall off. Let my tongue which will not sing stick to the roof of my mouth."

They are angry with the turncoats from Edom who cheered when Jerusalem was destroyed. They are furious with the Babylonians. "We hope someone gives you everything you dished out. We wish that someone would throw your children against the rocks."

The Hebrews sang this angry psalm during services commemorating the anniversary of the exile—their holocaust. They sang about children being smashed against rocks right there in worship.

Psalm 137 doesn't often get set to music—for good reasons. The psalms have inspired books with titles like *The Beauty of the Psalms* that print the text of psalms along with pictures of oceans, evergreens, and small children. They never include Psalm 137 with a picture of a rock garden. One of the best-selling books on Psalms is *A Shepherd Looks at the 23rd Psalm*. There is no sequel titled *A Babylonian Looks at the 137th Psalm*. The next time you are in a Christian bookstore, ask if they have any T-shirts with Psalm 137:9 printed on them.

In its exposition of the last verse of this psalm, the *Broadman Bible Commentary* says, "It remains startling in its cruelty. One almost wishes for such a line to be gone altogether." Almost? Bernhard Anderson writes, "It is surely legitimate to question whether the *whole* Psalter should be retained in Christian worship, [especially] this troublesome passage."

This psalm that starts so beautifully and ends so angrily is a gift to people like us. The Hebrew people sang this angry, violent, troubling song because they hurt like we do.

We avoid, evade, and sidestep our anger. We try to ignore the ways in which we have been hurt, but genuine faith is honest. Tears are as much a part of who we are as laughter is.

We should bring our emotions with us to God—especially whatever bitterness we feel. We should be honest about the heartaches we've known and slow to announce that everything is fine.

We know our share of Edomites and Babylonians: coworkers who don't do their part but claim credit for work we did; the employer who decides we are expendable; the neighbor who makes us feel small; the people who don't accept and fail to explain why; a mother who is too demanding or too submissive; a father who is in our face or out of the picture. Life is harsh.

We have good reasons to be angry: with those to whom we give our hearts only to discover that we shouldn't have; with daughters who don't recognize the love they've been given; with sons who grow up to curse their parents; with friends for whom betrayal seems second nature; with the one who commits suicide who should have known we would never be able to forget them; with the ones who die too soon.

Nobody lives long without scars. Everybody gets hurt. The grief and anger we feel is holy because it is honest. We don't want to be people who have learned not to cry or people incapable of rage.

We can be honest with God when we are hurting. When we share our lives with God, we remember what it feels like to hope. When we can't sing, we can still remember the song. We may not be able to stop grieving, but we can remember God's love.

The table is for hurting people who are willing to bring their heartaches to this supper. Communion is for those who know they get angry and need grace for life's hard journey.

At the table, we remember Christ whose heart was broken as he gathered his friends. The feast commemorates the suffering love of God. God invites everyone who has been hurt to say, "God, I've been carrying this sorrow around for a long time. It's hard for me to imagine not carrying this with me for the rest of my life. But at least I can share it with you."

INTENTIONAL WORSHIP

JOSHUA 24:1-27

Joshua said to the people, "See, this stone shall be a witness against us; for it has heard all the words of the LORD that he spoke to us; therefore it shall be a witness against you, if you deal falsely with your God." (Joshua 24:27)

He slips in just as the organist is beginning the prelude and glances at his watch. Why couldn't they start at 10:45? If they had a head start, they could beat the Methodists to Chili's. He likes the chiming of the hour. He thinks of it as the tardy bell that says you are officially late. He has never cared for the candles. They are a little too Catholic for his taste. He yawns during the reading of the psalm.

When the friendship register is passed, he writes other people's names. Over the last three Sundays, he has written "Emma Watson," "Stephen Colbert," and "Sasha Obama." Someone has to notice eventually. The first hymn seems like a high church hymn. That's why they have Episcopal churches. The second hymn sounds low church. That's why they have yuppie churches. During the children's sermon, he hopes some child will say something the pastor doesn't want to hear. It doesn't happen often enough.

He has never been big on litanies. He doesn't come to worship to participate, although the Lord's Prayer isn't bad. He is used to mumbling it. The anthem is a winner, but the Scripture reading goes on forever. Who reads twenty-seven verses from Joshua? Who cares about the Amorites, Perizzites, Canaanites, Hittites, Girgashites,

Hivites, and Jebusites? The text is long enough to make you long for John 3:16.

The sermon starts slow and drags in the middle, but he likes it when the introduction and conclusion are close together. He is sure the closing hymn is somebody's grandmother's favorite, but it isn't his. He looks at his watch and then around to see if anyone is going to join. He hopes new members will wait a week, because kickoff is at 1:00.

When the offering plate is passed, he gives money that he will not miss. He likes the *Doxology* because it's short and the benediction because it means the service is almost done. He leaves the sanctuary thinking, "It could've been worse."

Somehow he has gotten the mistaken impression that worship is a spectator sport. He has never understood that attending a worship service and worshiping are not the same. If you asked him why he comes, he'd have to think about it for a second. If it's to be entertained, it's not much of a show. If he wants to learn something, a book is easier. If he's after self-improvement, then therapy could be more useful. If he wants to feel comforted, then the Grand Slam Breakfast at Denny's might be a better choice. The truth is, more than anything else, he comes out of habit.

Old Testament preachers like Joshua didn't have much patience with worshipers like him. The world was a different place thirty-three centuries ago. Rivers parted so that people could walk across on dry land. The heroine in the book of Joshua is a prostitute. The major holidays were celebrated by making big piles of rocks. Capital punishment involved stoning not only the perpetrator but also his sons, daughters, cattle, donkeys, sheep, and tent.

The difference between the ancient Israelites and twenty-first-century Americans is clear in the moment when Joshua says to the Hebrew people, "This is it. You have to choose. Are you going to truly worship God?" We are not used to the idea that worship is such a big deal.

Joshua is a tough old bird. He is Rooster Cogburn shouting at Ned Pepper. When his fellow spies felt like grasshoppers and the Canaanites looked like giants, Joshua and his friend Caleb urged the

Hebrews to take them on, even when their more safety-minded compatriots threatened to stone them for their advice. After Moses died and Joshua assumed command, he showed his mettle by trusting God to bring down the walls of Jericho with only the sound of a trumpet and the shouts of the people.

When Joshua realizes that his days are numbered, he calls together the tribes of Israel at Shechem, where Abraham and Jacob built altars, for his farewell address. The Israelites are settling in the promised land, but their hearts are restless. Some are faithful to Yahweh, the God who led them through the wilderness. Others like the pagan religions that surround them. Most of them don't take worship seriously. With all the energy a 110-year-old can muster, Joshua challenges the people to renew their commitment to the one true God. He begins with a recitation of history.

God was with them in bringing Abraham from the land beyond the river to a new home, in leading them out of slavery in Egypt, in the peculiar business with the prophet Balaam and the talking donkey, in making room in the promised land, and in the holy hornet, the panic that helped them find a place.

The people must decide whether they will serve the gods of the people around them or the God who has been with them every step of the journey. Anyone who has been sharpening pew pencils has started paying attention. The time has come for them to make up their minds: "Choose for yourselves this day whom you will serve; as for me and my family, we will serve God."

Joshua extends the invitation, and the people respond overwhelmingly. Everyone walks the aisle. Most preachers introduce new members and invite everyone to come shake their hands, but not Joshua: "I don't believe you. You don't mean it. You can't do it. You don't have what it takes. If you choose God, you'll have to pay a price. You have to give everything you are to God."

Joshua is being honest when he tells them that faithfulness is hard. Responding to God requires the reordering of everything. Life with God takes determination. There can be no competing loyalties.

Joshua thinks they are taking a serious commitment lightly: "You'd better mean it. You have to put away everything that competes with God and give yourself completely."

The people say, "We promise."

So that they will remember what they have pledged in worship, they set up a stone, and Joshua says, "Every time you see this rock, remember that you've given your word."

Joshua got angry when people showed up at a worship service without any intention of real sacrifice. Can you imagine how Joshua would feel about what passes for worship today?

Several decades ago, church growth experts started pushing the concept of market-driven worship. The idea is that churches should cater to the consumer mentality. If silly skits, Hawaiian shirts, and Scripture-quoting plate spinners will pack more people in, then by all means get silly skits, Hawaiian shirts, and Scripture-quoting plate spinners.

People increasingly think of user-friendly worship services as a matter of personal preference. We shouldn't suggest that people pick a worship service in which they feel comfortable because, not surprisingly, most are more comfortable in a pep rally than in an encounter with the Holy God. Clapping is easier than asking God to change us.

Too much of what passes for worship is superficial: hugs that would bring sexual harassment charges in other settings, applause that seems to suggest that the true audience is not God but the congregation, the feeling that nothing mysterious is going on and that what is happening is a gathering of nice people enjoying one another's presence.

Those who lead worship are told to keep it simple. Do not ask soul-wrenching questions. Avoid anything that is offensive. Offer sweetness rather than the hard thinking that the Christian faith requires. Lots of people get just enough dumbed-down worship to inoculate them from experiencing the real thing. Consumer-driven worship leads people to the misunderstanding that worship is about our likes and dislikes and not about our commitment to God.

Worship is not supposed to be easy. If worship were easy, then everyone would worship.

Genuinely worshiping God is the most important thing we do. We need to bow down before God, rediscover our lives, be met by God's forgiveness, and see the vision of the day yet to come. God demands our lives.

She has had a hard week. She comes to worship to experience the love of God that makes her whole again. At the chiming of the hour, she looks at the cross at the front of the sanctuary and thinks about God's love. As the candles are lit, she asks God to help her worship. She listens intently as the psalm is read: "The children should set their hope in God." During the invocation, she closes her eyes, listens for God, and opens her heart.

She feels the hymns all the way down to her toes. The litany makes her think about the awesomeness of God. When she prays the Lord's Prayer, there is a lump in her throat on "forgive us our trespasses." She likes the part in the Scripture reading where Joshua tells the people of Israel, "Saying something doesn't make it so." As she listens to the sermon, she pictures herself faced with the choice the Hebrew people had to make. What holds her back from a greater commitment? What does it cost to truly worship God?

When the offering plate is passed, she gives more than her CPA wants her to because she knows she is not just giving money; she is sharing herself. She stands and praises "Father, Son, and Holy Ghost."

When she receives Communion, she thinks of it as receiving the strength she needs to live for God this week.

She is grateful for the benediction because it keeps her from hurrying back to life outside of worship. She lives differently because she has worshiped, because she has eaten the bread, because she has given herself to God.

WHAT DO WE MEAN WHEN WE SAY "GOD"?

EZEKIEL 36:22-32

A new heart I will give you, and a new spirit I will put within you; and I will remove from your body the heart of stone and give you a heart of flesh. I will put my spirit within you. (Ezekiel 36:26-27)

A grasshopper is sitting on a milkweed plant near the railroad tracks in Helena, Montana. The Great Northern Railroad goes by and the train creates a huge ruckus. The milkweed starts to bounce, bob, and weave. The grasshopper looks around. She has no idea what is happening. Something big is going on, but it is beyond the grasshopper's understanding. God is at least that incomprehensible. However we imagine God, God is bigger. That is why it is so hard to talk about God. To define God is to limit God.

Talking about God is so difficult that we shy away from it even at church. When we are asked, "How have you experienced God's presence this week?" most of us hope that someone else will answer.

Talking about God is hard because we are surrounded by self-centered secularism and crazy religion. We have either unbelieving humanists who think the idea of God is silly, or far-too-confident religious people who have God all figured out. If churches are not careful, the difficulty of talking about God becomes an excuse to be less interested in God than we are in the church.

When people talk about God, they usually don't stop to say what they mean when they say "God." The English word "God" has an equivalent in almost every language. Cherokees call God "The Great

Spirit." Hasidic Jews call God "The Master of the Universe." The Hindus believe that you can call God by any name, because there is no name that is not God's name. God has created every sound, so every sound names God.

When asked what they mean when they say God, some talk about the people around them. God is within us in the willingness to sacrifice for the common good. We see God in the faces of those who seem to have found the secret of joy. We see God in the compassion of a teacher, the persistence of a child, and the tenderness of a loving mother. Something of God is within us, and yet the Infinite God is far beyond us. God is inside our hearts, and God is more.

When asked to describe God, some would talk about the glory of nature. God is the rustling of leaves, the sound of the ocean, and the singing of birds. Looking into the heavens and not believing seems hard.

God is revealed in sky, wind, and rain. God is in the sunset, and yet God is bigger than the sunset. God is creation, and God is more.

When asked to define God, some talk about the mystical experience of God's presence. God is revealed in moments of oneness, connection, and communion when we rest in the hope that we are not alone.

In spiritual enlightenment, silence, and prayer, we know God's grace. God is the unity we feel, and yet God is beyond our feelings. God is the experience of holiness, and God is more.

Some of the most disappointing talk about God implies that God is a tool for self-improvement. God is the means by which we lose ten pounds, read more books, and have a good-looking lawn. We try so hard to be successful that we are tempted to see God as a means to get more done. God is how I will have a good marriage, raise good children, or enjoy my singleness. We act as if God is the servant of self-interests. In recent years, church has been dominated by a person-centered approach.

Our culture's individualism makes it hard to think about God as the focus of our understanding. The stories in Scripture seem peculiar, in part, because they speak primarily about God and only secondarily about us. Ezekiel believed that life is God-centered and not self-centered.

In 587 BCE, Babylon destroyed Jerusalem and forced Ezekiel and many of the Hebrew people into exile. From the Babylonian point of view, the defeat of Judah is proof of the worthlessness of Judah's God. Yahweh is unable to protect these people.

The Hebrews have doubts. God's chosen ones have been cruelly taken from their promised land. They have hit rock bottom when Ezekiel brings the word of God: "I will gather you together and bring you home."

When Ezekiel proclaims that God will deliver the people, he echoes a central theme of Scripture. Despair makes people of faith cling to the promise that God will take them home. What's surprising about what Ezekiel says is the reason he gives for God's deliverance: "'It's not for your sake, O house of Israel, that I'm about to act, but for the sake of my holy name, which you have profaned among the nations . . . . Through you I will vindicate the holiness of my great name . . . . It is not for your sake that I will act,' says the Lord God."

God will not deliver out of concern for the people. Israel has nothing to contribute to their deliverance. The people wait empty-handed to receive whatever God chooses to give.

Most prophets tell people to repent and live differently. Ezekiel says that what they do is beside the point. Their future rests solely on the hope that God will be God.

Walter Brueggemann says this text pictures God like a parent in a restaurant with small children. The children are tired and are not behaving well. The parents are exhausted and embarrassed. Not much is at stake for the children. They are behaving like children. Much is at stake for the parents. Everybody is watching. They might like to reprimand their children, but the people in the restaurant will think they are bad parents. They become models of patience because people are looking.

Ezekiel says that has happened to God. God's children have thrown one long tantrum. God has been the long-suffering, patient parent. Everyone is watching to see what God will do now that the people have pushed God too far. Here, at the end of the rope, there is no talk about repentance. There are no promises by Israel that they will do better next time. There is nothing left but God. The prophet says that God is too gracious to let people's foolishness stand in the way.

God is the ultimate reality on which all else depends. God is a verb as well as a noun, the power that keeps everything going, and the energy that flows through the universe. God is the breath inside all living things, the electric spark that charges our hearts, the fire inside the sun, the space between the stars, and the axis around which the galaxies spin. God is the eternal spirit who is the beginning and end of creation. God is an excessive, exuberant, playful whiz, an ingenious expert in higher math, and a frolicking, laughing, dancing God. God is the great "I Am" and the one revealed in Jesus.

Our hope is that God will gather us from all nations, races, and peoples and bring us home. God will offer us the bread of life and the cup of grace. God will give us a new heart and put a new Spirit within us. God will be God.

JUSTICE, KINDNESS, HUMILITY

MICAH 6:1-8

"God has told you, O mortal, what is good: and what does the Lord require of you but to do justice, and to love kindness, and to walk humbly with your God?" (Micah 6:8)

One morning in my eighth grade social studies class, the teacher said, "The world is one-third Christian, twenty percent Muslim, and thirteen percent Hindu."

We thought that was the goofiest thing we had ever heard. Where I grew up in Mississippi, there were four religions—Baptist, Methodist, Presbyterian, and heathen. Almost everyone we knew was a Christian. The small number of people who were not Christians had the decency to keep it to themselves. The idea that two-thirds of the people in the world are not Christians was hard to believe.

The statistics are not as hard to imagine as they once were. The world is getting smaller, and we are realizing that it's bigger than we thought. When I was in high school, my friends had names like Mark, Michael, Michelle, Jenny, and John. My son's friends include Machmud, Carlos, Ekta, Zoheb, and Anoosha.

There are Sikh communities in New York and Buddhist retreat centers in West Virginia. By one count, there are 1,650 different religious movements with at least 2,000 members in the United States. What should it mean to us that there are more than twice as many Sunni Muslims as there are Protestant Christians? We are in the minority, and the percentage of Christians gets smaller each year. We hear from a variety of religious viewpoints. Knowing how to respond is hard.

At the vacation Bible schools I attended growing up, Friday was decision day. The pastor presented the plan of salvation and invited us to be baptized. Most of us were baptized by the third grade. Some years we were invited to walk to the front. This led to kindergarten students making decisions as a group. The poor minister had to visit the homes of two dozen five-year-olds to tell their parents that their children wanted to be baptized. Many of those five-year-olds, now faced with the frightening prospect of actually being baptized, responded, "I only went because everyone else did."

The invitation was something like this: "We are all sinners. Jesus died on the cross for our sins. If we accept Jesus' sacrifice and pray for Jesus to come into our hearts, we will be saved and go to heaven when we die."

Some churches had a sixth grader who thought it was his job to ask, "But what about the Indians? They never even heard about Jesus."

Most pastors hate the "What about the Indians?" question. The hard-line response is, "The Indians are out of luck. They missed the boat. We're in and they're out."

We can find it comforting to believe that we are in and everyone else is out, but it doesn't seem right. Believing that God's grace is only for a small percentage of us is insulting to God. We recognize that if we had been born in Indonesia, then we would probably be Muslims. We wouldn't know many of the stories we've been taught or believe many of the truths we've learned.

If God is at work everywhere, then we should not dismiss the rest of the world as having nothing to say. God loves us too much to play favorites. We make a mistake when we try to divide the world into those who attend Christian churches and those who will never have a chance to know God's love.

There is, of course, an opposite mistake. When asked, "What about the Indians?" some respond, "Don't worry about the Indians, because deep down everyone believes the same thing." Saying that all religions are the same is popular, as if we could combine the great traditions into one big mess of a melting pot. The people who think that all religions teach the same truths haven't listened. Christianity, Islam, Hinduism, Buddhism, Judaism, Confucianism, transcendental meditation, materialism, numerology, astrology, scientology, and jogging say different things. When religious tolerance discourages the honest evaluation of beliefs, it also discourages commitment. Tolerance by itself is apathy. To say that all religions are equal is to say that no religion makes a real difference.

How should we feel about being a minority in a world filled with different religions? First, we should recognize that we are not the first to ask the question. While religious pluralism may be a new experience for those of us who grew up in Mississippi, it was the everyday experience of the Hebrew people. The Israelites were surrounded by the thousands of gods and goddesses that belonged to their neighbors. Sometimes they responded by destroying their neighbors, and sometimes they bought some of their idols just to be safe.

Seven hundred years before Christ, Israel is in the middle of a revival. The temple is crowded. The balcony is full. Giving is over budget. They have more programs than ever, but Micah knows that something is wrong.

The prophet pictures God charging Israel with a crime and taking them to court. God calls the mountains, hills, and foundations of the earth as witnesses for the prosecution. God's accusation is that they are selfish people who have forgotten God's generosity. God loved Israel, brought them out of slavery, and gave them a home. God speaks in pleading tones as a parent to a child who ignores the parent's love.

The people miss the point: "God, what more could you possibly want from us? Do you want more sacrifices, more expensive livestock? How about a thousand sheep? Just how religious can we be?"

Their idea of religion is far from God's hopes. They think that religion consists of believing the right things and staying away from the people who believe the wrong things. Appearing religious is easier than being kind.

"What does God want?" the prophet asks.

God wants us to do justice—to be a voice for the oppressed, the widow, and the foreigner.

God wants us to love kindness—to care for the handicapped, minorities, the elderly, and the poor.

God wants us to walk humbly with God—to listen for God's voice wherever God may be heard, learn how other people make sense of their lives, and thoughtfully examine what it means to live with faith.

We will be better Christians not if we put down every idea that is Muslim, Buddhist, or Hindu but if we affirm the truth and keep searching. We should not agree with everything, but we should recognize that Christians have much to learn as well as share. We should find ways to say, "I have something I want to share with you, and you have something I hope you'll share with me."

Some think that hearing other viewpoints will lead us to lose our faith, but that is not true for most. We become more mature Christians when we come to see that the great religions struggle with things that matter, express a real human experience, and deserve attention for the wisdom they offer the rest of humanity.

Could it be that sometimes whether we have the right answers is less important to God than whether we show compassion? Isn't that what Micah says?

The great enemy is the partial practice of faith. The religious tradition of which I want to be a part includes Elie Wiesel, Mahatma Gandhi, and Anwar Sadat. Do we have more in common with a person who says she is a Christian but has no real commitment or with the faithful member of another tradition who lives with God's kindness?

Christians should cling tenaciously to what we believe comes closest to truth, hold tightly to the story we have been given, test it, doubt it, try it, believe it, share it, and celebrate it.

In a world of countless religions, what should we do? We should do justice, love kindness, and walk humbly with God. Christ's table is open to all who will do what is just. The Eucharist is for those who do not take themselves as seriously as they take God.

Everyday Saints

Revelation 7:9-17

After this I looked, and there was a great multitude that no one could count, from every nation, from all tribes and peoples and languages, standing before the throne and before the Lamb, robed in white, with palm branches in their hands. (Revelation 7:9)

The late Gordon Cosby, a pastor in Washington, D.C., told of a middle-aged church member saying, "I'm not coming to church anymore. It isn't turning out like I thought it would. When I became a Christian, I was ready to lay down my life for Christ. I would have gone anywhere, done anything, paid any price—and you made me an usher."

We have had holy moments when we desperately wanted to live for Jesus. We felt like we had to feed the hungry and tell the story. We were sure we were going to do great things.

We thought we were going to slay dragons. Now it feels like we are getting pecked to death by ducks. Some days are dull. Some days are hard. Most days we are busy with other things. Life is not turning out like we dreamed.

About sixty years after Jesus' death and resurrection, life is not turning out like the church hoped. They were going to set the world on fire and be immortalized in stained-glass windows.

Christians become a tiny movement on the fringe of an evil empire, a fragile church hanging on by its fingernails, Russell Crowe with no sword and no gladiator suit.

The Roman emperor Nero persecutes Christians. The emperor Domitian enforces the worship of the emperor. Christians know that life is going to get even harder. Life is not turning out like they hoped.

From the Isle of Patmos, John tells them about his amazing vision. John writes that when the curtain is raised and the last act is revealed, there will be a great multitude from every nation, race, and language standing before the throne.

Christians who feel like they are alone are part of a choir so large that no one can count them. They sing, "Blessing, glory, wisdom, thanks, power, and might to God."

When John asks, "Who are these people?" God tells him that they are the ones who have been faithful. They kept believing, hoping, and giving. The great shepherd will wipe away their tears.

These saints are a great parade moving toward the throne of God: Abraham, father of Islam, Judaism, and Christianity, whose teenage son Isaac nonetheless stopped sending Father's Day cards for a while; Joseph—good dreams, good coat, bad attitude; Moses, who wondered at times if he should have stayed in Egypt and let Yul Bryner be in charge; Rahab, the kind of loving woman you do not want talking to your son; David, who had days when he wished Goliath had ducked; Mary, the mother of Jesus, who liked to look for the brightest star on cold winter nights; Nicodemus, who put up wind chimes; Peter, who hated the sound of roosters. They found something worth living for and gave themselves to it heart, body, and mind. They refused under any circumstances to be parted from it.

The church suffers from amnesia, forgetting those who have cleared the path on which we walk. We would not be here without the saints: Martin Luther—if there had been Prozac in the 1500s, he might not have started the Reformation; Pope John the 23rd, who changed the church Luther gave up on; Sojourner Truth, who insisted that she was free; Dietrich Bonhoeffer, whose discipleship was so costly; Lottie Moon, four foot three inches of Baptist preacher; Martin Luther King, Jr., who preached that justice should roll down like waters; Mother Teresa, who showed that righteousness is an ever-flowing stream; Mohandas Gandhi, who died because he dared to make peace; Bishop Oscar Romero, who was murdered while serving

Communion. And there are countless saints whom only God remembers, who relished life so much that they gave it away.

Saints give clothing away and pack sack lunches. Saints pray and teach Sunday school. They give money that they would rather keep. Some saints don't serve in soup lines but sit down at the table and enjoy their best meal of the week. Some saints don't give their clothing to Goodwill. They go to Goodwill looking for jackets for their children.

Most saints work outside the church walls: teachers who love second graders one spelling word at a time; hospice nurses who offer comfort to those who face the end; mothers and fathers who work at home because they feel God's invitation to live out their calling at their own address; counselors who listen to those to whom no one else listens; writers who share a word of grace with those who need a word of grace; high school students who tutor elementary school students; mechanics who do an honest job for an honest price; lawyers who forget which cases are *pro bono*; business people who hire workers on whom no one else will take a chance; saints in the rank and file of everyday life.

When we sing a hymn, read Scripture, or pray, we are doing so with the saints. We are dependent on those who have come before us to give us the words, tell us the stories, and teach us the tunes with which we find the way that leads to God.

In *The Power and the Glory*, Graham Greene tells the story of a seedy, alcoholic Catholic priest who after months as a fugitive is finally caught by the revolutionary Mexican government and condemned to be shot. On the evening before his execution, he sits in his cell with a flask of brandy to keep his courage up. He thinks back over the dingy failure of his life. Greene writes,

> Tears poured down his face. He was not at the moment afraid of damnation—even the fear of pain was in the background. He felt only an immense disappointment because he had to go to God empty-handed, with nothing done at all. It seemed to him at that moment that it would have been quite easy to have been a saint. It could only have needed a little self-restraint, and a little courage.

He felt like someone who had missed happiness by seconds at an appointed place. He knew now that at the end there was only one thing that counted—to be a saint. (*The Power and the Glory*, ed. R. W. B. Lewis and Peter J. Conn [New York: Viking Press, 1970])

Saints show us the only thing that counts. Our way may seem humdrum when compared with some, but we can live out of God's hope. When we take the bread and cup, we take our places before the throne and add our voices to the choir. We share in a song that was being sung long before we got here and will last for all eternity. We share the bread with a multitude who in every age witnessed to their faith in life and death, those for whom the trumpets sounded as they passed to the other side. We share the cup with those whom we have loved and who have gone to be with God, whose names are written on our hearts. God calls us to be saints together with those in every place who call on the name of Christ.

THANKSGIVING SUPPER

LUKE 24:14-34

A dispute also arose among them as to which one of them was to be regarded as the greatest. (Luke 22:24)

At 10:30 on Thanksgiving Day, I am standing in a long line waiting for a box of Thanksgiving. We are not in a restaurant, as you might expect, but in a nondescript building—a VFW hall, Rotary Club hall, or Jehovah's Witness Kingdom Hall. We stand in line in a plain, undecorated room waiting to say our last name and be handed our order by a woman who gives the impression that she has been sitting there several hours longer than she wants to. We are sent to a bigger, duller room to stand in a longer line. When we get to the front of this line, one of the dozen or so people handling orders fills a cardboard box with a turkey, a pan of dressing, a chocolate pie, and two bags of rolls. Along the wall there are dozens of boxes marked "choc" or "appl." As she puts in the rolls, I realize that I don't smell anything. In spite of the presence of several hundred Thanksgiving dinners, there is no Thanksgiving dinner smell because none of the food has been cooked there.

On Thanksgiving Day, this crowd doesn't seem thankful or even happy. An elderly man in a Boomer Sooner sweatshirt has his hood pulled up as if something vaguely disreputable is going on. The people there are embarrassed to admit that they didn't do their own basting, baking, boiling, broiling, roasting, and toasting. Their rolls rose in someone else's oven. How will they explain if someone sees them? "I know how this looks, but I swear this is our first time. We're so busy that we had no choice. What are you doing here, anyway?"

What we're doing is trying to buy a box of Thanksgiving—not just a turkey, dressing, pie, and rolls but the experience of a family Thanksgiving. Maybe the room is eerily quiet because we suspect that it isn't going to work. The fortunate ones of us remember Thanksgiving at Grandmother's house—the smells wafting from the kitchen, the constant questions about when the food will be ready, putting extra leaves in the dining room table, and setting up the card table in the kitchen. The view from the card table was not much, and Grandma's dressing was dry, but the memories smell better every year.

The pace of life has changed. Buying a box of Thanksgiving makes sense, and the turkey tastes fine, but it is hard to believe that thirty years from now our children will say, "I want a chocolate pie just like we used to pick up at the VFW hall."

As the time for the Passover draws near, Jesus hopes that everything will turn out just right. Leonardo da Vinci's painting of the Last Supper makes it seem idyllic. We might think that the Last Supper would qualify as a picture-perfect meal. Jesus goes to a lot of trouble for this thanksgiving dinner. This is his last chance to eat with his friends, so he prepares with great care. He chooses a guest room in Jerusalem and sends two disciples ahead to purchase bread and herbs, roast the lamb, and set the table.

As they begin to eat, Jesus tells them how much he has looked forward to sharing thanksgiving. He says that they are his family and tells them to "divide the cup among you." The supper is warm and wonderful: "Everybody on this side of the table for a picture." The meal is picture perfect for a while. But then Jesus shocks the disciples when he warns them of a traitor in their midst. He makes a final appeal to Judas, his friend of three years.

The disciples talk about what has become an ongoing betrayal. They argue over who is the most important. Jesus has addressed this on at least four occasions. No one knows how many times have gone unmentioned. He must have been tempted to throw up his hands in disgust. "What's the use? You're never going to get it."

Jesus turns his attention to Simon Peter. Satan is going to sift him like wheat. When Jesus most needs his friends, none of them are going to be there.

In the space of four paragraphs, Jesus eats this thanksgiving meal with his family, says that one of them is going to kill him, listens as they argue over who is the greatest, and sadly informs Simon that he will act like no friend at all. By the time the pumpkin pie is served, Jesus is alone.

In light of the pettiness, phoniness, and selfishness at the Last Supper, how can this table be thanksgiving? Jesus makes it clear that the Last Supper is not thanksgiving for where we are; it's for where we are going. Jesus tells his friends of a thanksgiving dinner yet to be. One day there will be a table with no pettiness, phoniness, or selfishness.

This is not the Last Supper so much as it is the promise of the Last Supper. At the end of it all, there will be a glorious thanksgiving dinner free of the deceit that was present at that first Last Supper and every succeeding one.

The family at the table has not changed much. Like Jesus' first disciples, we are not as brave as we should be, but our present failures will not keep us from being God's people. One day, we will live as God's family.

We give thanks for our destination. The supper that we celebrate is the appetizer. The table invites us to live in gratitude for the promise of what is yet to be. One day, we will gather around the table for a thanksgiving meal to end all thanksgiving meals.

HOW TO TELL YOUR STORY

You shall set it down before the Lord your God and bow down before the Lord your God. Then you, together with the Levites and the aliens who reside among you, shall celebrate with all the bounty that the Lord your God has given to you and to your house. (Deuteronomy 26:10-11)

How do you respond when someone says, "Tell us a little bit about yourself"? Most of us have trouble with this simple inquiry. How do we begin to tell the story of our lives? Telling your story seems simple until you start to do it. You find that it is not as easy as you thought. What do I tell? What do I leave out? How do I describe who I am? The challenge is not knowing the facts but understanding what they mean.

Learning to tell our stories is central to being a Christian. When we talk about faith, we are learning what to tell and what to leave out, what is important and what is not. We work to learn to tell our stories truthfully and see the framework with which to understand our lives. That is what is going on in the twenty-sixth chapter of Deuteronomy.

The harvest season is drawing to a close. Each worshiper comes into the sanctuary carrying a basket filled with fruit. They present their baskets to the priest, who sets them in front of the altar and then, of all the things that might happen after an offering—a prayer, the doxology, money counters coming to take it away—the worshipers tell their story: "A wandering Aramean was my ancestor. My father was Jacob, the father of us all, Jacob the rascal, Jacob who wrestled with God until dawn and was given a blessing. My father went to Egypt and there became a great people, but then Pharaoh made us his slaves. As we toiled all day under the hot sun, it seemed hopeless. We had no future, but we cried out to the God of our mothers and fathers. God set us free, brought us out of slavery, and led us to the homeland promised to our ancestors. We are grateful for what God has given."

They came to worship to tell the story of God giving them freedom and taking them to the promised land. The story is so familiar that we may not realize that they told it with amazing faith and understanding. In a sermon on this text, Patrick Willson, a retired Presbyterian minister in Albuquerque, pointed out that there are other ways in which this story could be told.

The Hebrew people could have made themselves the heroes of the story: "Our ancestors were strong and clever. We were once slaves in Egypt, but we refused to be kept down. We escaped and fought our way across the Sinai Peninsula. We wandered in the desert for years. Many died in the wilderness, but the best of us grew stronger. We finally came to the great cities of the Canaanites. We fought for years and triumphed because of our skill in battle. This land is ours because we took it with the sword and claimed it for our own. That's our story and we're proud of it."

This is quite a different way of telling the story. The events are roughly the same, but the storyteller understands it differently. Some people tell their story as though it is an achievement. We are tempted to make a list of what we have accomplished. We like to tell our stories as if we pulled ourselves up by our own bootstraps.

I grew up in the turmoil of the Deep South in the 1960s and the hardships of the rust belt North in the 1970s. I chose Baylor, a demanding school, the world's largest Baptist university. My parents wondered if I would have enough money to pay tuition—it was up to $45 a semester hour—but I took a grueling job in the bookstore, worked as many as eight hours a week, and I made it. I moved to Louisville, Kentucky, where I finished a Master's and a Ph.D. in only eight short years. I served as a pastor for twenty-two years in four churches that my mother would describe as prominent. In each place of service, I was respected by several people in the community. The fourth largest seminary in Atlanta thought I should be shaping young minds, so now I am one of the fifteen finest professors at McAfee.

Telling our stories that way is fun. I am what I have made of myself. My story is the story of my success.

There are a variety of ways to tell any story. You can tell a story without it meaning anything. How about this?

"Our ancestors were so lucky. When we were slaves in Egypt, we managed to sneak away, and luck was on our side. We got across the Red Sea in the dry season when the water was low. The chariots that tried to follow got stuck in the mud. We wandered in the desert for years almost starving, but even in the worst times good things just happened. In the nick of time, we found water. Food seemed to fall from the sky. When we reached Canaan, we hit the right place at the right time. The Egyptians to the south and the Hittites to the north were declining. The Assyrians were too weak and far away. The Philistines hadn't moved in yet. All we had to do was take over a few tiny Canaanite villages. The land just fell into our hands. We were really lucky. That's the story. It's no big deal."

The same events are barely held together. One thing happens, then another—random occurrences without meaning. Sometimes we tell our story that way.

I was born in South Dakota. I grew up in Mississippi and went to high school in Ohio. I graduated from college. Carol and I met in Louisville and got married. I took a job in Indiana. Graham was born. We moved to Kansas. Caleb was born. We moved to Waco, then Fort Worth, and now Atlanta. That's the story. It's no big deal.

All the facts are right, but it doesn't mean anything. Lots of people tell their stories without attaching any meaning to them. Their lives are a series of unconnected events without any great significance.

If we see our lives as meaningless happenstance or as the product of our own labors, then we have missed the point. How should we understand our stories? How do we make sense of them?

We start to find the meaning of our lives when we recognize that our stories began long before we arrived. The words in Deuteronomy were recorded by a community that had lived in Palestine for several generations. The Israelites taught their children this old story of God's grace to their ancestors because it was their story. The Hebrew people had lived in the promised land for a long time, yet they were still learning what it meant.

We are paragraphs in God's continuing story. William Bausch wrote, "Learning our story means learning the larger story of revelation, of God and God's movement in history. Then it means learning the smaller story of ourselves, of God's movement in our own personal history."

The Hebrew worshipers told their story with thanksgiving: "With a mighty hand and signs and wonders, God delivered us from slavery and brought us to this land flowing with milk and honey."

Every worshiper's story is the story of what God has given. Let me tell you my story. This time I will try to tell the truth. Way back in the beginning, before the bang that made matter and energy, there was the Mystery of God. God's goodness erupted and created the heavens and the earth. God made people to hear their stories. Through holy men and women, God told a story of love and justice. Two thousand years ago, my story took a dramatic turn in the story of Jesus. In Jesus' life and death, we see the heart of God broken and opened in front of us.

The people who loved Jesus' story became the church. They discovered that the Spirit was with them to help them remember and live the story. Our ancestors have tried and failed and tried again to get the story right. The best of the lot have not only been faithful to the story but have added to its glory.

Not many years ago at all, some people in Mississippi told the story to my grandparents who told it to my mother who claimed it as her story, too. A college student in Texas told the story to my father, who decided that he wanted it to be his story. My parents and those with whom they shared the story helped me slowly but surely begin to understand that my life has meaning in the light of the story.

Several churches encouraged me to explore God's gracious invitation to ministry. At seminary, I met a most genuine Christian. I was amazed that Carol would give me the time of day. In my lucid moments, I am still amazed. A church in Indiana cared for us through the tragedy of a miscarriage. When Graham and Caleb were born, we recognized that they were gifts of grace. We have served delightful churches filled with saints. Through those caring sisters and brothers, God has loved and taught me. Being part of the community at my seminary has been delightful. When I look at God's story and my story, the story is all about grace.

I don't come to Christ's table on my own. I come with everyone who has ever been to the table, because I haven't written my story on my own. I am dependent on everyone who shares the story. Our story is the story of God helping us find hope in a story bigger than our own.

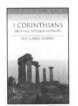

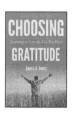

Choosing Gratitude
Learning to Love the Life You Have
James A. Autry

Autry reminds us that gratitude is a choice, a spiritual—not social—process. He suggests that if we cultivate gratitude as a way of being, we may not change the world and its ills, but we can change our response to the world. If we fill our lives with moments of gratitude, we will indeed love the life we have.   *978-1-57312-614-4 144 pages/pb* **$15.00**

Choosing Gratitude 365 Days a Year
Your Daily Guide to Grateful Living
James A. Autry and Sally J. Pederson

Filled with quotes, poems, and the inspired voices of both Pederson and Autry, in a society consumed by fears of not having "enough"—money, possessions, security, and so on—this book suggests that if we cultivate gratitude as a way of being, we may not change the world and its ills, but we can change our response to the world.   *978-1-57312-689-2 210 pages/pb* **$18.00**

Contextualizing the Gospel
A Homiletic Commentary on 1 Corinthians
Brian L. Harbour

Harbour examines every part of Paul's letter, providing a rich resource for those who want to struggle with the difficult texts as well as the simple texts, who want to know how God's word—all of it—intersects with their lives today.   *978-1-57312-589-5 240 pages/pb* **$19.00**

Dance Lessons
Moving to the Beat of God's Heart
Jeanie Miley

Miley shares her joys and struggles a she learns to "dance" with the Spirit of the Living God.   *978-1-57312-622-9 240 pages/pb* **$19.00**

A Divine Duet
Ministry and Motherhood
Alicia Davis Porterfield, ed.

Each essay in this inspiring collection is as different as the mother-minister who wrote it, from theologians to chaplains, inner-city ministers to rural-poverty ministers, youth pastors to preachers, mothers who have adopted, birthed, and done both.

978-1-57312-676-2 146 pages/pb **$16.00**

The Enoch Factor
The Sacred Art of Knowing God
Steve McSwain

The Enoch Factor is a persuasive argument for a more enlightened religious dialogue in America, one that affirms the goals of all religions—guiding followers in self-awareness, finding serenity and happiness, and discovering what the author describes as "the sacred art of knowing God." *978-1-57312-556-7 256 pages/pb* **$21.00**

Ethics as if Jesus Mattered
Essays in Honor of Glen H. Stassen
Rick Axtell, Michelle Tooley, Michael L. Westmoreland-White, eds.

Ethics as if Jesus Mattered will introduce Stassen's work to a new generation, advance dialogue and debate in Christian ethics, and inspire more faithful discipleship just as it honors one whom the contributors consider a mentor. *978-1-57312-695-3 234 pages/pb* **$18.00**

Healing Our Hurts
Coping with Difficult Emotions
Daniel Bagby

In *Healing Our Hurts*, Daniel Bagby identifies and explains all the dynamics at play in these complex emotions. Offering practical biblical insights to these feelings, he interprets faith-based responses to separate overly religious piety from true, natural human emotion. This book helps us learn how to deal with life's difficult emotions in a redemptive and responsible way. *978-1-57312-613-7 144 pages/pb* **$15.00**

Help! I Teach Youth Sunday School
Brian Foreman, Bo Prosser, and David Woody

Real-life stories are mingled with information on Youth and their culture, common myths about Sunday School, a new way of preparing the Sunday school lesson, creative teaching ideas, ways to think about growing a class, and how to reach out for new members and reach in to old members. *1-57312-427-3 128 pages/pb* **$14.0**

Hope for the Thinking Christian
Seeking a Path of Faith through Everyday Life
Stephen Reese

Readers who want to confront their faith more directly, to think it through and be open to God in an individual, authentic, spiritual encounter will find a resonant voice in Stephen Reese.

978-1-57312-553-6 160 pages/pb **$16.00**

A Hungry Soul Desperate to Taste God's Grace
Honest Prayers for Life

Charles Qualls

Part of how we *see* God is determined by how we *listen* to God. There is so much noise and movement in the world that competes with images of God. This noise would drown out God's beckoning voice and distract us. Charles Qualls's newest book offers readers prayers for that journey toward the meaning and mystery of God.   *978-1-57312-648-9 152 pages/pb* **$14.00**

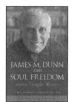

James M. Dunn and Soul Freedom
Aaron Douglas Weaver

James Milton Dunn, over the last fifty years, has been the most aggressive Baptist proponent for religious liberty in the United States. Soul freedom—voluntary, uncoerced faith and an unfettered individual conscience before God—is the basis of his understanding of church-state separation and the historic Baptist basis of religious liberty.   *978-1-57312-590-1 224 pages/pb* **$18.00**

The Jesus Tribe
Following Christ in the Land of the Empire

Ronnie McBrayer

The Jesus Tribe fleshes out the implications, possibilities, contradictions, and complexities of what it means to live within the Jesus Tribe and in the shadow of the American Empire.

978-1-57312-592-5 208 pages/pb **$17.00**

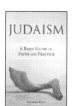

Judaism
A Brief Guide to Faith and Practice

Sharon Pace

Sharon Pace's newest book is a sensitive and comprehensive introduction to Judaism. What is it like to be born into the Jewish community? How does belief in the One God and a universal morality shape the way in which Jews see the world? How does one find meaning in life and the courage to endure suffering? How does one mark joy and forge community ties?   *978-1-57312-644-1 144 pages/pb* **$16.00**

Lessons from the Cloth 2
501 More One Minute Motivators for Leaders

Bo Prosser and Charles Qualls

As the force that drives organizations to accomplishment, leadership is at a crucial point in churches, corporations, families, and almost every arena of life. In this follow-up to their first volume, Prosser and Qualls will inspire you to keep growing in your leadership career.

978-1-57312-665-6 152 pages/pb **$11.00**

Let Me More of Their Beauty See .
Reading Familiar Verses in Context

Diane G. Chen

Let Me More of Their Beauty See offers eight examples of how attention to the historical and literary settings can safeguard against taking a text out of context, bring out its transforming power in greater dimension, and help us apply Scripture appropriately in our daily lives.

978-1-57312-564-2 *160 pages/pb* **$17.00**

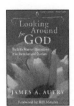

Looking Around for God
The Strangely Reverent Observations of an Unconventional Christian

James A. Autry

Looking Around for God, Autry's tenth book, is in many ways his most personal. In it he considers his unique life of faith and belief in God. Autry is a former Fortune 500 executive, author, poet, and consultant whose work has had a significant influence on leadership thinking.

978-157312-484-3 *144 pages/pb* **$16.00**

Making the Timeless Word Timely
A Primer for Preachers

Michael B. Brown

Michael Brown writes, "There is a simple formula for sermon preparation that creates messages that apply and engage whether your parish is rural or urban, young or old, rich or poor, five thousand members or fifty." The other part of the task, of course, involves being creative and insightful enough to know how to take the general formula for sermon preparation and make it particular in its impact on a specific congregation. Brown guides the reader through the formula and the skills to employ it with excellence and integrity.

978-1-57312-578-9 *160 pages/pb* **$16.00**

Meeting Jesus Today
For the Cautious, the Curious, and the Committed

Jeanie Miley

Meeting Jesus Today, ideal for both individual study and small groups, is intended to be used as a workbook. It is designed to move readers from studying the Scriptures and ideas within the chapters to recording their journey with the Living Christ.

978-1-57312-677-9 *320 pages/pb* **$19.00**

The Ministry Life
101 Tips for New Ministers
John Killinger

Sharing years of wisdom from more than fifty years in ministry and teaching, *The Ministry Life: 101 Tips for New Ministers* by John Killinger is filled with practical advice and wisdom for a minister's day-to-day tasks as well as advice on intellectual and spiritual habits to keep ministers of any age healthy and fulfilled. *978-1-57312-662-5 244 pages/pb* **$19.00**

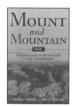

Mount and Mountain
Vol. 1: A Reverend and a Rabbi Talk About the Ten Commandments
Rami Shapiro and Michael Smith

Mount and Mountain represents the first half of an interfaith dialogue—a dialogue that neither preaches nor placates but challenges its participants to work both singly and together in the task of reinterpreting sacred texts. Mike and Rami discuss the nature of divinity, the power of faith, the beauty of myth and story, the necessity of doubt, the achievements, failings, and future of religion, and, above all, the struggle to live ethically and in harmony with the way of God. *978-1-57312-612-0 144 pages/pb* **$15.00**

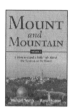

Mount and Mountain
Vol. 2: A Reverend and a Rabbi Talk About the Sermon on the Mount
Rami Shapiro and Michael Smith

This book, focused on the Sermon on the Mount, represents the second half of Mike and Rami's dialogue. In it, Mike and Rami explore the text of Jesus' sermon cooperatively, contributing perspectives drawn from their lives and religious traditions and seeking moments of illumination. *978-1-57312-654-0 254 pages/pb* **$19.00**

Overcoming Adolescence
Growing Beyond Childhood into Maturity
Marion D. Aldridge

In *Overcoming Adolescence*, Marion D. Aldridge poses questions for adults of all ages to consider. His challenge to readers is one he has personally worked to confront: to grow up *all the way*—mentally, physically, academically, socially, emotionally, and spiritually. The key involves not only knowing how to work through the process but also how to recognize what may be contributing to our perpetual adolescence.

978-1-57312-577-2 156 pages/pb **$17.00**

Psychic Pancakes & Communion Pizza
More Musings and Mutterings of a Church Misfit
Bert Montgomery

Psychic Pancakes & Communion Pizza is Bert Montgomery's highly anticipated follow-up to *Elvis, Willie, Jesus & Me* and contains further reflections on music, film, culture, life, and finding Jesus in the midst of it all. 978-1-57312-578-9 *160 pages/pb* **$16.00**

Quiet Faith
An Introvert's Guide to Spiritual Survival
Judson Edwards

In eight finely crafted chapters, Edwards looks at key issues like evangelism, interpreting the Bible, dealing with doubt, and surviving the church from the perspective of a confirmed, but sometimes reluctant, introvert. In the process, he offers some provocative insights that introverts will find helpful and reassuring. 978-1-57312-681-6 *144 pages/pb* **$15.00**

Reading Ezekiel (Reading the Old Testament series)
A Literary and Theological Commentary
Marvin A. Sweeney

The book of Ezekiel points to the return of YHWH to the holy temple at the center of a reconstituted Israel and creation at large. As such, the book of Ezekiel portrays the purging of Jerusalem, the Temple, and the people, to reconstitute them as part of a new creation at the conclusion of the book. With Jerusalem, the Temple, and the people so purged, YHWH stands once again in the holy center of the created world.

978-1-57312-658-8 *264 pages/pb* **$22.00**

Reading Hosea–Micah
(Reading the Old Testament series)
A Literary and Theological Commentary
Terence E. Fretheim

Terence E. Fretheim explores themes of indictment, judgment, and salvation in Hosea–Micah. The indictment against the people of God especially involves issues of idolatry, as well as abuse of the poor and needy. The effects of such behaviors are often horrendous in their severity. While God is often the subject of such judgments, the consequences, like fruit, grow out of the deed itself. 978-1-57312-687-8 *224 pages/pb* **$22.00**

Reading Samuel (Reading the Old Testament series)
A Literary and Theological Commentary

Johanna W. H. van Wijk-Bos

Interpreted masterfully by preeminent Old Testament scholar Johanna W. H. van Wijk-Bos, the story of Samuel touches on a vast array of subjects that make up the rich fabric of human life. The reader gains an inside look at leadership, royal intrigue, military campaigns, occult practices, and the significance of religious objects of veneration.

978-1-57312-607-6 272 pages/pb **$22.00**

Sessions with Genesis (Session Bible Studies series)
The Story Begins

Tony W. Cartledge

Immersing us in the book of Genesis, Tony W. Cartledge examines both its major stories and the smaller cycles of hope and failure, of promise and judgment. Genesis introduces these themes of divine faithfulness and human failure in unmistakable terms, tracing Israel's beginning to the creation of the world and professing a belief that Israel's particular history had universal significance.

978-1-57312-636-6 144 pages/pb **$14.00**

Sessions with Revelation (Session Bible Studies series)
The Final Days of Evil

David Sapp

David Sapp's careful guide through Revelation demonstrates that it is a letter of hope for believers; it is less about the last days of history than it is about the last days of evil. Without eliminating its mystery, Sapp unlocks Revelation's central truths so that its relevance becomes clear.

978-1-57312-706-6 166 pages/pb **$14.00**

Silver Linings
My Life Before and After *Challenger 7*

June Scobee Rodgers

We know the public story of *Challenger 7*'s tragic destruction. That day, June's life took a new direction that ultimately led to the creation of the Challenger Center and to new life and new love. Her story of Christian faith and triumph over adversity will inspire readers of every age.

978-1-57312-570-3 352 pages/hc **$28.00**
978-1-57312-694-6 352 pages/pb **$18.00**

Spacious
Exploring Faith and Place
Holly Sprink

Exploring where we are and why that matters to God is an ongoing process. If we are present and attentive, God creatively and continuously widens our view of the world. *978-1-57312-649-6 156 pages/pb* **$16.00**

The Teaching Church
Congregation as Mentor
Christopher M. Hamlin / Sarah Jackson Shelton

Collected in *The Teaching Church: Congregation as Mentor* are the stories of the pastors who shared how congregations have shaped, nurtured, and, sometimes, broken their resolve to be faithful servants of God. *978-1-57312-682-3 112 pages/pb* **$13.00**

A Time to Laugh
Humor in the Bible
Mark E. Biddle

An extension of his well-loved seminary course on humor in the Bible, *A Time to Laugh* draws on Mark E. Biddle's command of Hebrew language and cultural subtleties to explore the ways humor was intentionally incorporated into Scripture. With characteristic liveliness, Biddle guides the reader through the stories of six biblical characters who did rather unexpected things. *978-1-57312-683-0 164 pages/pb* **$14.00**

This Is What a Preacher Looks Like
Sermons by Baptist Women in Ministry
Pamela Durso, ed.

In this collection of sermons by thirty-six Baptist women, their voices are soft and loud, prophetic and pastoral, humorous and sincere. They are African American, Asian, Latina, and Caucasian. They are sisters, wives, mothers, grandmothers, aunts, and friends. *978-1-57312-554-3 144 pages/pb* **$18.00**

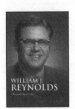

William J. Reynolds
Church Musician
David W. Music

William J. Reynolds is renowned among Baptist musicians, music ministers, song leaders, and hymnody students. In eminently readable style, David W. Music's comprehensive biography describes Reynolds's family and educational background, his career as a minister of music, denominational leader, and seminary professor. *978-1-57312-690-8 358 pages/pb* **$23.00**